With Ash on Their Faces

With Ash on Their Faces

Yezidi Women and the Islamic State

Cathy Otten

OR Books

New York · London

© 2017 Cathy Otten

Published for the book trade by OR Books in partnership with
Counterpoint Press.
Distributed to the trade by Publishers Group West.

First printing 2017

Cataloging-in-Publication data is available from the Library of Congress.
A catalog record for this book is available from the British Library.

ISBN 978-1-944869-45-8

Text design by Under|Over. Typeset by AarkMany Media, Chennai, India.

10 9 8 7 6 5 4 3 2 1

For my Mum and Dad

Table of Contents

If there were water we should stop and drink
Amongst the rock one cannot stop or think
Sweat is dry and feet are in the sand
If there were only water amongst the rock
Dead mountain mouth of carious teeth that cannot spit
Here one can neither stand nor lie nor sit
There is not even silence in the mountains
But dry sterile thunder without rain

—T.S. Eliot, *The Waste Land*

God witnessed this tragedy,

the stunned moon witnessed it,

the lithe xerophytes witnessed it,

the salty warm dark soil witnessed it,

the hot golden noon witnessed it,

the burned houses, the dead bodies,

the dusty air, the blood's smell,

and the sunbeams witnessed it.

But, none dared to prevent it.

I did not: coward, feeble, poor sister.

—Nawaf Ashur, "Five Sisters"

Glossary

KRG   (Kurdistan Regional Government) has governed the semi-autonomous Kurdistan Region in northern Iraq since the no-fly zone was put in place after Saddam Hussein's brutal repression of the 1991 Kurdish uprising. The Kurdistan Regional President Masoud Barzani has ruled for over ten years and his term has been extended twice. His nephew Nechirvan Barzani is the Prime Minister of the Kurdistan Region, and his son Masrour Barzani is the Chancellor of the Kurdistan Region's Security Council.

KDP   (Kurdistan Democratic Party), founded in 1946, is one of the two main parties in the KRG, and is led by acting KRG President Masoud Barzani. The KDP's power base is in Erbil and Dohuk governorates in the west of the Kurdistan Region. Dohuk shares a border with Turkey and the KDP has good relations with Turkey's ruling party.

PUK   (Patriotic Union of Kurdistan), founded in 1975 after splitting from the KDP, is the other main political party in the KRG, with a strong support base in Sulaimaniyah and Kirkuk provinces, and eastern areas of the Kurdistan Region. The PUK, unlike the KDP, has traditionally had closer ties with the PKK, Iran and the Iraqi federal government. The KDP and PUK fought a civil war between 1994 and 1998.

PKK (Kurdistan Worker's Party) was established in 1978 and is led by Abdullah Öcalan. The PKK has fought the Turkish state in a war for Kurdish rights and more autonomy which has lasted over three decades and resulted in more than thirty thousand dead on both sides. The PKK, classified as a terrorist organization by the EU, US, and Turkey, has bases in the mountains where Turkey, Iran, and Iraq meet.[1]

YPG (People's Protection Units) is the armed force that protects the autonomous cantons known as Rojava in northern Syria that emerged out of the tumult of that country's civil war. The YPG is an affiliate of the PKK, but unlike the PKK it is not listed as a terrorist organisation and benefits from security co-operation with the US in the war against ISIS.

YBS (Shingal Resistance Units) is a local Yezidi force that falls under the PKK umbrella and also includes many YPG and PKK fighters in its ranks.

HPE (Êzidxan Protection Force) is an independent Yezidi force in Sinjar led by Hayder Shesho. The force briefly received salaries from the Iraqi government. In 2015 Shesho was detained and then released by the KDP on charges of commanding an unsanctioned militia. His force is now reportedly under the Ministry of Peshmerga.

ISIS is the Islamic State in Iraq and Syria, previously known as the Islamic State of Iraq (ISI). ISI grew from the ashes of Al-Qaeda in Iraq (AQI) after the death of its leader, Abu Musab al Zarqawi, in a US drone strike north of Baghdad in 2006. In 2013, ISI split with the Al-Qaeda franchise when it announced that it would rule the Syrian Al Qaeda branch and become ISIS. In June 2014 the group changed the name to Islamic State. It is also commonly known as ISIL, Daesh, IS (Islamic State), or ISIS.

Peshmerga is the army of the Kurdistan region, which grew out of long-standing guerrilla fighters of the KDP and PUK. They are split into three main groups: the KDP-aligned 80 force, the PUK-aligned 70 force, and 14 Regional Guard

Brigades administered by the KRG's Ministry of Peshmerga. Recently the Peshmerga have also absorbed smaller Yezidi militias. Reform plans call for Peshmerga professionalization under unified non-partisan command. In Kurdish, Peshmerga means "those who face death."

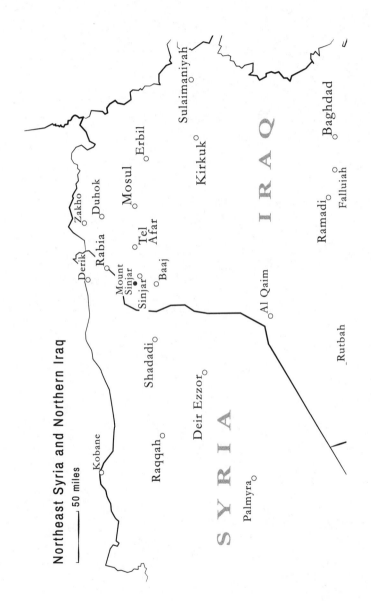

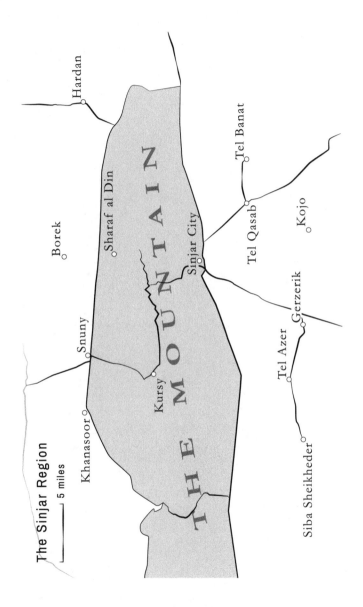

The Sinjar Region

5 miles

THE MOUNTAIN

Hardan

Borek

Sharaf al Din

Snuny

Khanasoor

Kursy

Sinjar City

Tel Banat

Tel Qasab

Kojo

Gerzerik

Tel Azer

Siba Sheikheder

Introduction

It was a bright, early autumn morning outside the psychiatric ward of a hospital in Iraqi Kurdistan. Sunlight doused the corridors. Outside the windows, the mountains that divide Iraq, Turkey, and Syria were still topped with snow. Inside, lining the hallways, were people who had made it this far to ask for help.

The psychiatrist, Dr. Haitham Abdulrazak, couldn't offer them much in the way of medicine (the hospital's stocks were low). Instead, he talked with his patients, attempting to find out more about the events that lay behind their symptoms. He allowed me to watch and report. I observed Yezidi survivors delivering anxious, staccato reports about their experiences of escape and murder.

Dr. Haitham, a tall, stooping man with a bright yellow shirt under his doctor's jacket, spoke to them softly. After the worst years of the civil war in Iraq, he had left his position at a clinic in Baghdad to come to this hospital in the town of Zakho, near the Turkish border in northern Iraq. The violence had followed him.

In the summer of 2014, about a third of Iraq fell to ISIS. Zakho, along with other towns and cities in the relatively safe Kurdistan region, were flooded with hundreds of thousands of desperate people. They were survivors of sudden massacres that had left thousands of corpses strewn across the plains of Sinjar.

Now these people were sleeping outside, in school playgrounds, parks, abandoned tower blocks, half constructed malls, and by the roadsides. Exhausted, traumatized, and with all their possessions lost, they were at least safe.

For most, the struggle to survive in such chaotic displacement was all-consuming. But, still, many who could afford the taxi ride made their way to Dr. Haitham's clinic. One young Yezidi woman lay in a catatonic state, her hands clenched in hard, rigid claws, her eyes staring fixedly, seeming to ask questions that no one could answer. Why did this happen to us? What did we do?

Another young woman was breathing rapidly and suffering from disassociation, Dr. Haitham said. She believed that her four-year-old sister, shot to death as they ran from their hometown as it was attacked by ISIS, was still alive. Dr. Haitham patiently asked her about herself and what had happened.

One of the most vital roles Dr. Haitham performed, it seemed to me, was to listen to his patients' stories without much interjection or judgment, but rather with understanding and empathy.

--

The killings and mass rapes targeting the Yezidis were not events that stood apart from history. The Yezidis had already been made vulnerable by forced displacement under Saddam Hussein, economic meltdown under UN sanctions, the breakdown of the state and security after the US-led invasion of 2003, and political failures that followed.

"Not all violence is hot. There's cold violence, too, which takes its time and finally gets its way," Teju Cole wrote in his essay "Letter to Palestine."

Around the world, a broader kind of cold violence continues. It's the violence of indignity, of forgetting, of carelessness and of not listening. It's there in the way politicians talk about refugees, and in the way the stateless are sometimes written about and photographed by the western media. It's there in the fear of outsiders—so central to the right-wing populism of the Brexit and Trump campaigns. It's there in the way humans dismiss other humans as less worthy of protection or care.

When cold violence and hot violence merge, we get the "perfect storm" of genocide, of mass killings inflicted on the most vulnerable.

Yezidis were not the only group to suffer the failings of the Iraqi state and fall prey to ISIS. ISIS has predominantly killed Muslims: thousands of Shia Iraqis were massacred and Sunni Muslims accused of treachery were executed in large numbers, too. Women were denied freedom and Christians were forced from their homes, robbed and their churches were bombed. Christians were killed in a series of deadly explosions and militant attacks in the years after the US-led invasion of 2003, which caused hundreds of thousands of Christians to flee Iraq.

Yezidis have suffered massacres and oppression for generations. But there was something different about the ISIS attack that took place in the late summer of 2014. This time the western media took notice. The plight of the Yezidis of Sinjar, in exodus from genocide, stranded starving on a mountain surrounded by ISIS, rapidly garnered widespread coverage and was cited by the US for its first overt engagements against ISIS in Iraq.

Many of the stories about the abduction and enslavement of Yezidi women and children describe them as "sex slaves," and feature graphic, sometimes lurid, accounts told by newly escaped survivors. Female fighters of Kurdish militias helping to free Yezidis from the mountain became fodder for often novelty coverage. The Yezidis became the embodiment of embattled, exotic minorities against the evil of ISIS.

This narrative has stereotyped Yezidi women as solely passive victims of mass rape at the hands of perpetrators presented as the embodiment of pure evil. While rightly condemning the crimes, this telling doesn't leave room for the context and history from which the violence emerged, or allow for further questions about why people act or don't act, why they and, by extension, we, do the things we do.

--

I moved to Iraqi Kurdistan in early 2013 from Manchester in the UK where I grew up, studied English Literature, and worked in a museum and as a freelance journalist for *The Big Issue North.* I moved to the city of Sulaimaniyah and met a group of Kurdish journalists and photographers who were (and still are) telling their own stories about their country and its people. It was a time of hope and renewal, with a postwar economic boom in Kurdistan. But, looking back, it's clear the events that would rock us all a year later, shattering the lives and livelihoods of so many people across Iraq, were already in motion.

When the Iraqi city of Mosul fell to ISIS in June 2014, half a million people fled to Iraqi Kurdistan. Many others remained and were trapped. Many of my Kurdish friends were personally affected. There was now a front line between ISIS and the military forces of the autonomous region of Iraqi Kurdistan. The new situation brought back stark memories of earlier attacks by Saddam Hussein's armies, when the Kurds had lost so much. Most families in Iraqi Kurdistan have at least one relative who was killed in prior wars with the Iraqi state. My friends shared stories about fleeing their homes as refugees and trekking through the snow and ice across the mountains with their families, on their way to camps in Iran. Thousands of Kurds had been gassed or executed in these earlier attacks. Now, the ghosts of the past re-emerged.

I suddenly felt out of my depth and, at the same time, a tragic incident related to the war profoundly shook my group of friends. For me, this tragedy was compounded by the loss of my home and a feeling of sudden isolation. In grappling with these events, against the advice of friends and family and in a state of numbness, I moved from Sulaimaniyah to Erbil, the capital of the Kurdistan region. From there, I wrote about the thousands of people fleeing from the ISIS attacks, which were happening in the towns across the Nineveh plain, forty miles from Erbil.

On August 3, 2014, Sinjar province had been attacked by ISIS and more than one hundred thousand people had fled to take refuge on a nearby mountain. Those that couldn't flee were rounded up. Many of the men were massacred while the women were enslaved. So many people were missing that the enslavement of women didn't immediately come to international attention.

Less than a week after they attacked Sinjar, ISIS surged toward Erbil and the local defenses collapsed. ISIS overran a camp of displaced people who had already fled from Mosul, including Iraqi army soldiers and police. My neighborhood in Erbil now became home to fifty thousand displaced people who were in shock, without medicine, food, and water, homeless in near fifty-degree (Celsius) heat.

From that time I remember: ghost-like people walking the streets of the city, desperate crowds gathering around places where limited aid was being distributed, highways entirely devoid of traffic, the ISIS flag fluttering ominously on the roadside in the south of Kirkuk city, and chaos and rumors mixing with the smell of bodies, hunger, and pain.

When US air strikes began that week, there was little standing between ISIS and the capital of Iraqi Kurdistan, where I now lived.

--

My interest in this topic came from following the story of Amal, who, along with her friend, was one of the first Yezidi girls to escape from having been kidnapped by ISIS. By now I was covering the war as a freelance reporter for *The Independent*. For that paper's Sunday magazine, I went with Amal on her first journey back to Sinjar Mountain after her escape. There she met female fighters and got as close as she could to the home she had lost. I saw her family offer prayers and gifts for her dead brother, who was murdered on the same day that Amal was captured.

I accompanied Amal when she visited the Yezidi religious leaders and described to them the difficulties she had encountered on her return and how these were eased by community acceptance after her rape. They were supportive of her.

At the age of eighteen, Amal was trying to put her life back together and, though she was in obvious pain, she also displayed courage and strength.

A little while later Amal was on the way to Germany with a program that offered psychological care and education to more than one thousand Yezidi female survivors. We met at a hotel in Erbil just before her departure. She was anxious about leaving, and grieving for her lost brother. She showed me his picture and began to cry.

Amal didn't enjoy her stay in Germany and missed her family. She returned not long after. I went to see her again while I was reporting for this book. By now she was working as a photographer and continuing to defy expectations about female victims and survivors. For her, the attack by ISIS had sharply ruptured the typical life of a young woman in her community and the Yezidi religion had to change and adapt to meet the needs of returning women like her.

It was only much later in my reporting on the return of the Yezidi women that I became aware of how important stories of captivity and resistance were to dealing with returning and dealing with trauma, both historically and in relation to ISIS. Yezidism is a closed religion and identity, one that is passed down through generations by stories and music. These practices have been extended to dealing with the traumas of the ISIS genocide.

Welcoming back survivors from ISIS, I heard women

in camps singing and retelling stories handed down from the responses to older conflicts. From these historical persecutions, Yezidi women remembered lessons such as rubbing ash onto their faces to become undesirable to their captors.

Though this book engages extensively with this history of storytelling as a means of promoting survival and resistance in the face of captivity, it does so without claiming that the practice is always successful. The telling of individual stories can seem to offer redemption, but it can also work to hide ongoing political failures that prevent redress and renewal and can even lead to further violence.

The failures are broad and deep. At the time of writing, Iraqi forces, backed by coalition air cover, are poised to rid Mosul of ISIS. Civilians have been killed by ISIS as they tried to flee, as well as being bombarded by Iraqi forces and the coalition. In March 2017 a US air strike on a house where families were sheltering in western Mosul killed more than one hundred civilians. Attention will then likely move from Iraq to the presence of ISIS in Syria. As Iraq's politicians and their military patrons prepare to congratulate themselves, the Yezidi community looks on from displacement camps, rented homes, or forced asylum overseas. Almost two years after it was cleared of ISIS by Kurdish forces, Sinjar city itself remains in ruins. A new wave of fighting for Sinjar province is under way, with Turkey eyeing a violent incursion after bombing the area in April. The idea that this represents "liberation" is seen by Yezidis as a bad joke. The UN and others have tried to recognize and document the genocide, but justice looks a long way off.

Meanwhile, the battle for survival of the women and girls who were taken by ISIS continues long after their return.

--

In *Night Draws Near,* the late Anthony Shadid wrote that "Journalism is imperfect. The more we know as reporters, the more complicated the story becomes and, by the nature of our profession, the less equipped we are to write about it with the justice and rigor it deserves."

This book is the work of one person from a country with a violent colonial history in Iraq, and with undoubted ingrained biases and perspectives. I've tried to make this account fair and balanced. There were of course limits to my research and reporting. There were interviewees I couldn't access and people's perspectives I haven't reflected. No doubt some people will feel they have not been fully represented. But my intention here was not to tell a full history of a people, or even to speak on behalf of the Yezidis who will continue to tell their own stories. Instead this is a narrative based on more than one hundred interviews about the ISIS attack in August 2014 and its aftermath, and especially on the impact it had on the women who were captured and taken away from their homes.

Most of the interviewees appearing in these pages spoke to

me while still suffering from the distress caused by their captivity and from conditions of ongoing displacement. For them, the events described here are not over but are rather part of an evolving and still traumatic history, and were at different times, I was told, painful and cathartic to recount.

In writing this book I worked with a group of Yezidi translators who speak the Sinjari dialect of Kurdish. Where needed, translations were cross-checked and accounts of events have generally been multiply sourced. When this wasn't possible, for instance with some accounts about captivity, they've been checked against each other and outside sources to evaluate veracity.

Some details in the accounts can't be independently confirmed and consideration of the impact of trauma on memory must be allowed for, and indeed can also be part of the narrative. The names of the survivors have been changed to protect their identity and are marked with quotation marks on first use.

I've tried to work in a way that doesn't cause further harm, by listening, particularly to ISIS survivors, most of whom are dealing with PTSD; by emphasizing choice in participation with this project; and by trying to avoid unhelpful stereotypes.

Cathy Otten, May 2017

A car carrying "Leila" drew close to her family's home in a camp for displaced Yezidis in northern Iraq. Her female relatives, dressed in black and brown shawls, sat around the sides of the room chatting in quiet voices. Next to the door was a small kitchen unit and, beneath it, a pile of black sandals to be slipped on before the women went outside onto the muddy roads of the camp.

It was midafternoon on an early spring day, just after a rainstorm, and outside the air was fresh and mountain-bruised. I asked the women where they were from. "Kojo," one of them gave me.

A few moments later everyone turned toward the door. They had heard car wheels crunching on the gravel outside.

Leila entered the room and collapsed into an older woman's arms. They began to cry. A small girl with pigtails ran in behind her, looking bewildered.

Leila wore a cream headscarf, a long black skirt, and a denim coat that was too big for her. Her face was red and scrunched up with tears washing her cheeks. The women wailed as she was carried into the room clutching her grandmother's breast. Everyone was crying now and the grandmother began to sing. The relief that Leila and the small girl had returned was tangible. But in the grandmother's mournful song there was also a lament for the women still held captive, and deep grief for the men from their village who had been murdered.

--

Leila sank into a corner of the room surrounded by a dozen members of her extended family who were gathering to receive her, women with olive skin and tired eyes. Each woman bent down to touch Leila and kiss her cheeks, welcoming her back. Her grandmother continued to sing.

Leila had been kidnapped a year and a half previously, taken from Kojo, a village below Sinjar Mountain. Her captors took her across two countries and then kept her locked in a house more than three hundred miles away, before she was able to escape.

She had been enslaved by ISIS, the militant jihadi group that captured large parts of Syria and Iraq in 2014 and embarked on a policy of exterminating the Yezidi religion, killing its men and taking its women into slavery because of the tenets of their interpretation of Islam.

The genocide is still ongoing and has only partially been revealed.

An estimated 6,383 Yezidis—mostly women and children—were enslaved and transported to ISIS prisons, military training camps, and the homes of fighters across eastern Syria and western Iraq, where they were raped, beaten, sold, and locked away. By mid-2016, 2,590 women and children had escaped or been smuggled out of the caliphate and 3,793 remained in captivity.[2] Around three thousand Yezidis were killed, half executed in the days following the ISIS attack, with the rest left dying on Sinjar Mountain from injuries, starvation, or dehydration.[3]

Some, like Leila, escaped by outsmarting the men, using methods of resistance passed down from earlier generations of Yezidi women who had endured religious persecution. Today over three thousand Yezidi women and children remain in captivity, where they've been since they were kidnapped in 2014, with few attempts to rescue them.

Leila's jailer, Shakir Abdul Wahab Ahmed Zaater, was an ISIS military commander in Rutbah, Anbar province, who became notorious after being filmed executing Syrian truck drivers in 2013.

"Where were you in Syria?" a neighbor asked the small girl accompanying Leila, who I later found out was her niece. She smiled up at her but didn't say anything.

As word of Leila's return spread around the camp, more women arrived to see her. They wanted to ask if she had news about their own missing relatives. As the crying in the room ebbed, one woman continued to weep loudly. Leila's grandmother told her to hush, and the women sniffed into silence. From the corner of the room, a teenage girl glanced up at me from under her black scarf, a fleeting look of relief on her face.

--

Leila is a Yezidi. The Yezidis are a majority-Kurdish-speaking religious group living mostly in northern Iraq and numbering less than one million worldwide. They worship a single God, believe in reincarnation, and revere the peacock angel, known as Melek Tawuse, as God's representative on earth. The peacock angel was often miscast as the devil of other religions, which resulted in the Yezidis, throughout their history, being persecuted as infidels by Muslim rulers who demanded they convert.

In Iraq there are around five hundred thousand Yezidis, primarily from the Sinjar region. Sinjar is a rural area in Iraq's Nineveh province, close to the border with Syria on the large, dry Jazira plain. Communities of Yezidis still exist in the Caucasus, but the Yezidis of Syria and Turkey have mostly all fled to neighboring countries or to Europe. In Germany, their numbers are estimated at twenty-five thousand.[4]

Sinjar was retaken by Kurdish forces backed by coalition air strikes in November 2015. The cost of its liberation was its near total destruction. The majority of Yezidis are still unable to return because of the ruination, and because they fear new clashes between the Kurdish militias who retook the area from ISIS, and were, at the time of writing, fighting with each other for control.

The epicenter of the Yezidi faith is in Lallish, not far from the city of Dohuk in Iraqi Kurdistan. Lallish is made up of a collection of temples set in a forested valley around the tomb of the Sufi mystic Sheikh Adi ibn Musafir, who died in the twelfth century and is revered by Yezidis. Every Yezidi must make a pilgrimage to Lallish at least once in his or her lifetime.

Sheikh Adi was born in Lebanon but came to Baghdad and then north to Lallish where he established a Sufi order, and was said to have mystical powers. Generations after his death, his followers began to incorporate elements of older, Iranian religions into their faith, meaning they would no longer be protected as part of the wider Islamic community.[5]

Yezidis believe that God created the universe from a pearl that split on his command and gave out light and water. He created seven holy beings or angels who he put in charge of making the earth, starting with Lallish. Melek Tawuse, the peacock angel, became their chief.[6]

The shrines in Lallish are dedicated to Sheikh Adi and his companions, real historical figures in the early years of the religion who have now become mythic. Praying to them, for modern Yezidis, cures illness and provides luck.

Yezidism is an oral religion, passed down through hymns sung by specially designated singers and the playing of holy instruments. Rather than formal ceremonies, religious practice involves visiting sacred places and kissing the walls of shrines and temples. Yezidis participate in baptism and feasts, sing hymns, and recite stories.

Some of the stories are about historical and mythical battles fought in protection of the religion. Others, told over the centuries by generations of women, detail methods of resistance to the same threats that Yezidi women face today.

"It is in our nature, we always want to survive, and then it depends on the having the knowledge to be able to do that," said Jan Kizilhan, the German-Yezidi professor of psychology and psychotherapy. "We call this trans-generational trauma.... Because the Yezidis have experienced 74 genocides, this information [on how to survive] is stored in their collective memories... they know their ancestors faced the same thing."

The stories are about suffering but also of strength. The relevance of these stories to the ISIS attacks, like the lament sung by Leila's grandmother, may help to redefine what it means to be Yezidi and create bonds that could offer some hope.[7]

Yezidi refugees first arrived in Sinjar in the early Ottoman period due to persecutions farther east near the town of Sheikhan, where the group's religious leaders are based. A stone tablet at the Sharaf al Din temple on Sinjar Mountain dates its foundations to the late thirteenth century. They were attracted by the protection the local Sinjar Mountain offered, and used the natural fortifications it provided as a base for rebellions against the Ottoman governors of nearby Mosul who wanted the Yezidis to pay taxes, join the army, and convert to Islam. [8]

Yezidis have suffered seventy-four separate genocides, which are remembered in their folklore, including a massacre by the Kurdish chieftain of Rowanduz in 1832, and another by Ottoman Lieutenant General Omar Wehbi Pasha fifty years later when hundreds of Yezidis were killed, villages robbed and destroyed, and the Yezidi prince was forced to convert to Islam.[9]

In 1837, the governor of Diyarbakir, Hafiz Pasha, and his troops surrounded Sinjar Mountain to get back booty stolen by Yezidi looters. The fighting lasted for three months. Yezidi fighters ran out of ammunition and had to surrender, emerging from the caves where they had been hiding. The governor retrieved the stolen goods, and took a number of Yezidi women

captive, who were then sold on the Mardin slave market, 115
kilometers northwest in present-day Turkey, for between $4.50
and $30.[10]

Dr. Frederick Forbes, who visited Sinjar a year after the
Hafiz Pasha attack, described the Yezidis sitting up until midnight around a large fire in the hills, "smoking and singing a kind
of lament for the taking of Sinjar, in which the name of Hafiz
Pasha was introduced at the end of each verse."[11]

--

Wadhah is a sixty-four-year-old Yezidi woman, who is now living
in the US as a refugee. She was raised on a farm near Sinjar by
parents who migrated south from what is now Turkey in 1919,
when an alliance between their tribe, the Denadi, and a local ally
of the Sultan broke down.[12]

Wadhah remembers being held in her mother's arms in the
garden and listening to stories the women told about how they
had escaped from their villages near what is now the southern
Turkish city of Sanliurfa, during the fall of the Ottoman Empire.
They fled toward the end of the Armenian Genocide, which
began in 1915, when 1.5 million Armenians were killed, and
Yezidis and other minorities were also targeted.

Sinjar stood at the Empire's southern reaches, which meant
there was less administrative and military pressure on its people,
and the town became a sanctuary for minorities, who were being

persecuted as the Ottoman Empire came to a violent end. The Mountain's topography and the complexity of its tribal fabric meant clashes were rarer there than in the towns and villages to the north.[13]

When the Denadi's alliance with the local emissary of the Ottoman sultan broke down, the Yezidi tribesmen feared for their lives. Wadhah's mother recalled watching as the men ran to hide when the gendarmerie arrived. She rubbed her face with ash so she would look unappealing and avoid being captured. This tactic was also used by Armenian women fleeing genocide years earlier.

Later, when the men of the town were killed en masse, including Wadhah's grandfather, the women and children fled to Sinjar on the backs of their donkeys. The children struggled to stay upright as they rode donkeys across the Jazira desert to Sinjar. Wadhah's grandmother gave birth to her father in a field along the way. Where the borders of Iraq, Syria, and Turkey meet now, caravans of refugees sheltered in temporary camps, fleeing the violent breakdown of order.

Nearly one hundred years after they sought shelter in Sinjar, Wadhah and her family were forced to flee again, this time from ISIS.

--

Iraq came under a British mandate after the collapse of Ottoman rule and remained so until 1932. At the end of the mandate, the dispute over the Iraq–Syria border was settled after investigation by a League of Nations boundary commission. The Yezidis of Sinjar remained in Iraq but the land of the Arab tribes was split between the two countries.[14]

Within living memory, Sinjar Mountain was covered in orchards of figs and grapes, fresh water springs, and herds of animals grazing. Even as the war with ISIS pummelled the city to the south, it was still possible to buy strings of dried figs and honey produced on the Mountain in the markets of northern Sinjar.

Mud brick houses and some small shops selling beer and snacks cling to the road above valleys filled with terraced tobacco fields, though the larger villages and water systems were all long ago destroyed. The tobacco leaves are hung to dry in the open air and rolled up in paper and smoked by the men, and some women.

Around the Mountain are a series of shrines that are said to date back to the thirteenth century, such as the Sharaf al Din temple, one of the most important in the Sinjar area. Like the shrine in Lallish, it's topped with a distinctive, ridged conical domed roof. Yezidis consider Sharaf al Din to be almost as important as Lallish and it remains a special place for newlyweds to come and be blessed.

At the top of the valley is the temple of Shebel Qassem, and in its yard is the grave of Hamu Shiro, a Yezidi resistance leader famous for sheltering Christian refugees during the First World War. By 1916, around nine hundred refugees had arrived in Sinjar fleeing killings and persecutions by the Ottomans and some Kurdish tribes farther north.[15]

Shamoon Hani, a Syrian Orthodox Christian, was one of those new arrivals. His grandchildren remember his story. After fleeing his home near Mardin, he found shelter with the Yezidis of Sinjar. When the global flu pandemic hit a few years later, villagers began dying and the Christian refugees were blamed for bringing the virus. Hamu Shiro intervened and allowed them to stay. These were the same years that Wadhah's parents and the Denadi tribe arrived.

One hundred years later, when ISIS attacked, Shamoon's grandchildren fled Sinjar, side by side with the descendants of their Yezidi rescuers. Now Shamoon's grandsons are back keeping bees on the Mountain and making honey with Yezidi tribesmen, mere miles away from the front line with ISIS.

Overlooking Hamu Shiro's grave is a tree mottled with small, knotted scraps of colorful fabric that flutter gently in the wind, tied by Yezidis who are hoping to have children. Beyond the tree are the graves of Yezidi soldiers killed fighting in the Iran–Iraq war of the 1980s, and the fresher graves of Yezidis killed by ISIS while defending Sinjar, and women and children who escaped the overrun city only to die of thirst and starvation under the unyielding August sun.

--

At the Mountain's southern base, below a winding road of hairpin bends, lies Sinjar city. The city was home to eighty thousand, including Yezidis, Christians, Sunni and Shia Muslim Kurds, Turkomen, and Arabs, before it was attacked and destroyed.[16]

Thama Ahmed, forty-eight, a Muslim from Sinjar, remembers how the city's different communities celebrated holidays and special occasions together. He showed me a black-and-white picture of his father in 1969, teaching at a primary school filled with Yezidi children. Thama's family grew figs in the city's orchards, not far from the old, leaning minaret where they would celebrate Newroz, the Kurdish spring festival.

The minaret was built as part of a madrasa by the governor of Mosul in 1202 AD during the late Abbasid period. Its circular tower was covered in geometric star patterns and inscriptions from the Koran. It suffered from the ravages of time, but was restored by the Iraqi State Board of Antiquities and Heritage in the 1960s.[17] ISIS would later destroy it.

Thama's house in Sinjar's old town was flattened in the fighting. He fled to ISIS-controlled Mosul, and then in late 2016 escaped again to a tent in the Kurdistan Region when the fight to retake Mosul was raging around him. The old town, a cluster of orange and brown mud brick buildings, rises on a series of low hills above the river. Thama showed me pictures of men sitting under the shade of olive trees by the river, surrounded by long grass and wild flowers. "Sometimes when it rained on the Mountain, the water would flow down to the town and we would find antiques and gold coins in the river," he said.

"I've got goose bumps thinking about Sinjar," said another Muslim man from the town, now living in a refugee camp. "I would cry if it wasn't so shameful."

In early 2014, Sinjar was peaceful and its atmosphere civil, even if its streets felt a little remote to passing visitors. Palm trees lined the roads, and in the bazaar small shops sold clothes, groceries, and shoes. Local men, some wearing the long, fur-lined robes that are traditional in the wintertime, strolled or sat together, smoking, talking, and drinking glasses of dark, sweet black tea that tinkled as the men stirred the liquid. Arabic could be heard on the streets—but other languages, such as Kurdish, Syriac, and Turkmen, were spoken there, too, by Nineveh's diverse population.

The red, green, and yellow flag of Iraq's Kurdistan Region hung from the old minaret.

One quiet April day in Sinjar's old town, a visitor knocked on the door of a Syriac church. The building was closed, but on the roof was a small, thin cross that would still be visible years later, even after the church had been destroyed. On the day the invaders came, the building was still surrounded by high walls; high walls that would do little to stop ISIS.

Part I:
The Fall of Sinjar

Chapter 1

"You are under our protection"

The day before ISIS came was a holiday in Sinjar. Yezidis gathered to celebrate the end of a fasting period named in honor of Sheikh Adi. It was the second day of August in 2014. Harvested wheat fields stood short and stubbly under the shadowless sun.

People slaughtered sheep and gathered with their relatives to celebrate the holiday, handing out sweets and exchanging news and gossip. In the past, they would have invited their Muslim neighbors to join the celebrations, but more recently distance had grown between them, leading the villagers to keep mostly to their own.

The atmosphere was restless and the temperature peaked above 104 degrees Fahrenheit. The top of the Sinjar Mountain appeared to be shimmering in the heat, and the people living below mostly avoided traveling until after the sun had set, when the streets were filled with neighbors trading fearful rumors, and men patrolling with guns.

At dusk, unfamiliar vehicles started to appear. The lights of the cars could be seen moving around out in the desert beyond the villages. A sense of foreboding grew as darkness fell. The Yezidi men took their guns and set out to check the horizon beyond the wheat fields, peering toward the outlying villages. On their return, they went back and gathered in the town center in small, tense groups.

Convoys of cars, kicking up dust in the distance, had appeared two months before, right before the city of Mosul, and the provincial capital, fell to ISIS. Mosul is 120 kilometers east of Sinjar, and its seizure was quickly followed by the fall of Beiji, Tirkit, and nearby Tel Afar. Four divisions of the Iraqi army collapsed, including the third division, which was based around Sinjar and included many Yezidis. The area was almost completely defenseless.

When they seized Mosul, ISIS freed the Sunni Muslims from the city's Badoush prison and set about executing six hundred Shia prisoners, considered apostates by the militants. The group plundered weapons and equipment from Iraqi army bases. Soldiers scattered their uniforms, and half a million civilians fled north and east to the Kurdistan Region. In the months before ISIS seized the city, Kurdish officials said they had warned the

Iraqi Prime Minister, Nouri al-Maliki, that terrorists were planning to overrun Mosul.[18]

The Yezidis were caught by surprise as city after city, town after town, were quickly captured. Within a week, a third of Iraq was under ISIS control. Sinjar district, with a population of around three hundred thousand, was surrounded. Only a thin strip of contested road remained linking them to the relative safety of the Iraqi Kurdistan in the north—but the journey was dangerous.

The Kurdistan region in northern Iraq is autonomous, and guarded by the Peshmerga, who now had to defend the three Kurdish provinces against ISIS. *Peshmerga* means "those who face death," and the word is heavy with the historical import of the Kurdish struggle against oppression, of martyrdom, and of bravery.

In the southeast, on the Iranian border, part of the Peshmerga clashed with ISIS, but near Sinjar, an uneasy stillness hung in the air like a tension headache that comes before a storm. Frantic rumors circulated. ISIS declared the birth of their caliphate across Syria and Iraq. Mosul, a city of around one million people, was its crown.

--

On Saturday, August 2, 2014, Jameel Choner, forty-nine, a former school teacher from the town of Borek, north of Sinjar Mountain, was entertaining friends at his home to celebrate the holiday; the conversation, however, was not festive. His guests were talking about what they should do about the escalation of the war around them. Some argued that the war was just between the Sunni and Shia Muslims and would pass them by, but Jameel felt uneasy.

Later that night he picked up his Kalashnikov and went to join a village meeting, something he would never normally do. There, he met a friend who told him that only four members of the Peshmerga were guarding the road leading north that stretched off into Sunni Arab farmland. News spread that Zummar, a mixed town between Sinjar and the rest of Kurdistan, was already under heavy ISIS attack.

"If anything happened we expected it would come from that direction because on the south side it was all Yezidis until the Mountain," Jameel remembered. Peshmerga were the only force present. The Iraqi army had collapsed. Sinjar was now an island in a desert of caliphate. Jameel and his friends had every reason to feel scared. They were surrounded.

By the early hours of August 3, rumors started to circulate that Sinjar's southern border was under attack. Jameel tried to call his friends but the phone lines were jammed.

--

Sinjar Mountain is circled by a string of towns and villages inhabited mostly by Yezidi farmers who, despite the lack of water and harsh landscape, manage to grow wheat and barley, and graze sheep. Some of the villages are older but eleven towns around the Mountain were built in the 1970s by Saddam Hussein's Baath regime, as part of an effort to control the Yezidis. Beyond the villages is Sunni Arab farmland.

Following the failed Kurdish uprisings of the mid-1970s, Saddam feared another Kurdish insurrection. Some of the Yezidis had fought with the Kurdish guerrillas against him, so he destroyed their villages and forcibly displaced them to new, concrete towns dotting the plains below. The Yezidis were prevented from speaking Kurdish and forced to register as Arabs.

Kurds number over thirty million worldwide and mostly live across Iran, Turkey, Iraq, and Syria. They are minorities in each country and have regularly suffered persecution and killings. The Yezidis were displaced as part of the larger program of Arabization, when Saddam forcibly moved a quarter of a million Kurds and resettled their land with Arabs from other parts of Iraq.

The new Yezidi towns were supposed to offer modern infrastructure, but also brought the Yezidis closer to the reach of the central government, and so were easier to rule. The towns, known as collectives, were generally laid out along a soulless grid with one- or two-story cream and brown buildings.

Toward the end of the Iraq–Iran war in the 1980s, Saddam killed one hundred thousand Kurds (some estimates are higher), destroyed thousands of villages, and used chemical weapons against them as part of a genocidal campaign.[19] In 1991 his regime brutally suppressed a Kurdish uprising, causing a Kurdish exodus to Iran and Turkey. In the aftermath, the US, Britain, and France set up a no-fly zone that allowed de facto Kurdish autonomy, although Sinjar remained under federal control.

The UN imposed sanctions on Iraq after the 1991 invasion of Kuwait. Ordinary Iraqis, who were still reeling from the losses of the Iran–Iraq war, paid a high price. Iraq's GDP shrank, oil production sharply declined, wages fell, prices shot up. Hyperinflation gripped the country.[20] The education system collapsed and the growing Iraqi middle class was devastated.[21]

Sanctions increased poverty dramatically and basic foodstuffs became scarcer. Smuggling oil, cigarettes, and livestock along the border was now even more lucrative and appealing. Meanwhile, Iraqi society became more religious, as Saddam tried to cement his rule after the disasters of the '80s and early '90s by fusing state Arab nationalist ideology with Islamism.[22]

--

When Mosul fell to ISIS on June 10, 2014, the Iraqi Army was riddled with corruption and had a ghost soldier problem. Senior officers were paid off so soldiers didn't have to turn up for duty. Initially, some people, chafing from years of abusive policing and arbitrary arrests, welcomed ISIS as liberators from the Shia-led government.

At the end of June, ISIS declared the establishment of their caliphate, and days later, the group's leader, Abu Bakr al-Baghdadi—an Iraqi from the city of Samarra and a former

US detainee—delivered a sermon during Friday prayers at Mosul's Great Mosque. Mosul's Christian communities were given the option to convert, pay a tax, or face death. Instead they fled, following thousands of other Christians who had already left during the last ten years of violence in Iraq.

Sinjar was now surrounded by ISIS, and by civilians who wouldn't be able to stand in the group's way. The road to the Kurdistan region was a thin sliver through hostile territory, and was barely controlled by the Peshmerga who prevented the Yezidis from fleeing to the Kurdistan region for shelter. "There is no danger . . . you are under our protection," Yezidis were told as they were turned back at the checkpoint by the Tigris River.

The only people who could pass into the Kurdistan region were those with doctor's notes or student IDs. Abu Haji, a driver from Sinjar, sensing the coming danger, snuck his family out one by one as he drove back and forth, hiding them between his regular passengers.

On August 2, a man from northern Sinjar was driving on a road that runs west of the Mountain, near the Syrian border, when he came to a checkpoint and stopped. He looked back toward the border and saw a line of dust kicked up by a convoy of vehicles moving through the desert. "What's that in the distance?" he asked the Peshmerga guarding the checkpoint.

It was ISIS. They were just 150 meters away.

Chapter 2

"We fought for six hours and nobody came"

Siba Sheikheder, southeast of Sinjar, is the closest Yezidi town to the Syrian border, a collection of a few hundred squat buildings. After 2003, the town marked the edge of Kurdish Peshmerga control. It was the site of a huge suicide car bombing in 2007 that killed hundreds of people.

When ISIS swept across the border earlier in the summer of 2014, they captured twenty-four Yezidi border guards. The men were imprisoned in Syria and threatened with death before being ransomed back to their families. Murat, forty-five, from Siba Sheikheder, was one of them, and he returned mentally broken and nearly destitute after paying the ransom.

Just before sundown, the people of Siba Sheikheder met to talk through a plan. Together with the village elders, they decided that no one would be allowed to leave. No matter what happened they would stay and fight.

The village elders were certain that the Peshmerga would back them up, recalled "Ali," a thirty-five-year-old who has keen blue eyes and chain-smoked thin cigarettes while we talked. He attended the meeting, and remembered that afterward, the fear grew more intense. Some of their Sunni neighbors in nearby villages called to warn the Yezidis that an attack was imminent.

"We were one hundred percent sure that they would attack us on that night," Ali said. "We knew."

The meeting ended at 9:20, just before sunset that evening. One hour later Ali saw a convoy of five cars coming through the desert. They stopped two kilometers west of the village with their headlights off. Next, a convoy of trucks approached from the south where the desert stretched off toward Anbar province, a Sunni Arab heartland.

A line of perhaps fifteen or sixteen vehicles now stood in the darkness, alarmingly close to Siba Sheikheder. The villagers felt surrounded. Yezidi men started calling Kurdish officials in Sinjar and were told that it was coming. "When people saw the convoys everyone went to the front lines to protect the town," Ali said. The front line had been reinforced around Siba Sheikheder after the town was attacked by jihadists in 2007.

On August 14 that year, militants detonated four truck bombs in Siba Sheikheder and neighboring Tel Azer, killing over five hundred people, wounding more than one thousand, and destroying four hundred homes. The bombings were the deadliest during the entire post-2003 war in Iraq. The explosions were so huge that many bodies were never found and families continue to carry photos of missing loved ones with them, hoping for news.

A woman from Tel Azer lost her twenty-four-year-old son in the attack. He was working in a shop near the site of one of the blasts. In the aftermath, dust and bodies were everywhere. She watched as bulldozers tried to uncover corpses buried in the rubble.

This attack came amid many killings of Yezidis and other groups, a cruel way to undermine the new order in Iraq that came to power after Saddam was deposed. After 2003, the threat from extremists became so severe that the Yezidis risked death if they tried to travel to Mosul, which is majority Sunni Arab, but also had Kurds, Christians, Shias, Yezidis, Shabak, and Turkmen. Hundreds of Yezidi families fled from Mosul to Kurdistan, and by November 2006, only a handful of Yezidi families remained.[23]

In spring 2003, US-led forces took control of Iraq in a matter of weeks, on the pretext of seizing stockpiles of Saddam's weapons of mass destruction that later turned out not to exist. That May, the US Coalition Provisional Authority assumed power and set about ordering the dissolution of Saddam's Baath party, barring its members from public roles, and disbanding Saddam's security services, including the army.[24]

"The adverse effects of these two decisions were to be felt for years to come," wrote historian Charles Tripp. "They put some 300,000 armed young men out of work at a stroke, stopped the pensions of tens of thousands of ex-officers and purged the slowly recovering government ministries of roughly 30,000 people, including their most experienced administrators."[25]

This sudden dissolution followed years of sanctions during which the Iraqi state had been severely weakened. The country was engulfed in violence and criminality. Looting was rife and thousands of Iraqis were killed. Into this milieu, a violent insurgency began among dispersed members of the former armed forces and Baathist rejectionists, which became mixed in with Islamists and foreign jihadi fighters.[26]

The missteps of the Americans during the occupation, including their failed economic and political policies, only empowered cronyism and corruption. US contractors benefitted instead of Iraqis whose everyday lives were upturned.[27]

Saddam had severely persecuted the majority Shia Muslim population during his rule, as he had done with the Kurds. After 2003, these groups were able to move into power and stake their claim on the new Iraq. A new paranoid class of out of touch, former exiles rose to power. They prioritized sectarian and opportunist politics, and were empowered by US diplomats holed up in Baghdad's fortified Green Zone.

In the north, the Kurds moved to control areas they had long claimed such as Kirkuk, Sinjar, and other parts of Nineveh province that had been Arabized by Saddam. This created a new and bitter line of opposition to Kurdish rule among non-Kurds, and enflamed tensions between Erbil and Baghdad, with both governments laying claim to the areas and their resources.

Combined with the rise of the insurgency and general breakdown of security, the new trigger line made Sinjar a focal point for increasing killings, kidnappings, and attacks. Mosul, which was known as a religiously conservative city of army officers, briefly fell to Sunni insurgents in late 2004.

In early 2005, Iraqis went to the polls to vote for a national assembly that would draft their new constitution. Insurgents threatened the vote and it was boycotted by many Sunni Arab politicians and voters. The winners were the Shia Islamist and Kurdish majority blocs. Later that year, Sunnis did come out and vote in the general election but the Shia and Kurdish parties still dominated, and in May 2006, Nouri al-Maliki, a Shia who joined the dissident Islamic Dawa party and then went into exile, became Prime Minister of Iraq.

After 2003, Yezidis got jobs with the Kurdish political parties and the Peshmerga, as well as with the Iraqi army, or traveled north to work as day laborers in Kurdistan. The Kurdistan Democratic Party (KDP) became the main political and security force in Sinjar. The second party, the Patriotic Union of Kurdistan (PUK), was also present.

Under the Baath regime, Yezidis had been pressured to iden-tify, and in some cases register as Arabs; but as Kurdish (KDP) control in Sinjar grew, the Yezidis were encouraged to identify as Kurds.[28] The Kurdistan Regional Government (KRG) sees the Yezidis as ethnically Kurds, and therefore Sinjar as rightfully part of the Kurdistan region. Yezidi identity was put into play by both sides to claim territorial control. In the violent post-2003 years Yezidis preferred being part of Kurdistan because of the insurgency plaguing the rest of Iraq.

The Kurdistan Region is primarily made up of Erbil, Dohuk, and Sulaimaniyah governorates, and is separated from Sinjar by Arab Iraq, which is partly why the Yezidis found themselves cut off in 2014. In the years after 2003, Kurdistan went through an economic boom. Officials signed oil contracts, the standard of living grew, and the region was largely peaceful.

In Sinjar, the KDP bartered for Yezidis' votes through patronage, which included access to employment, education, and healthcare, as well as preferential treatment at security check-points and in local-level administration.[29] This was explained to me by an anonymous UN political worker, who added that this also led to the increasing vilification of Arab tribes brought in through Arabization, their status and land ownership viewed as illegitimate.

The system had many benefits for Sinjar and the Yezidis, as the party invested in infrastructure, gave women more access to employment, built Yezidi cultural centers, increased access to Kurdish language education, and helped with the upkeep of shrines. The Dohuk governorate also shipped goods and supplies to Sinjar to avoid a humanitarian crisis when other trade routes for food, fuel, and construction materials were made inaccessible by an insurgent blockade.[30]

Over time the Kurdistan region supplanted Mosul as Sinjar's primary trading partner, increasing alienation from the city.

While the KDP was benefitting Yezidis, Al-Qaeda in Iraq was putting pressure on Sunni Muslim communities and offering them a means of retaliation, said the UN worker, not just against Kurdish hostility but also against wider de-Baathification laws in Iraq, which were seen to target Sunni Arabs.[31]

A visitor to Sinjar city on a rainy, cold day in early 2014 recalled that the local mayor's office was surrounded by blast walls and that the security atmosphere was tense.

To enter the town, it was necessary to pass through checkpoints of the KDP-aligned security forces. In his office, the mayor displayed a picture of himself with the head of the KDP branch, Serbest Baiperi. In the photo, the two men could be seen walking together and the mayor spoke about the head of the KDP office with reverence. The visitor saw the Kurdistan region flag hanging from the minaret in the old city, and felt that

Kurdish political culture was somewhat at odds with the more complex and heterogeneous culture of the city.

Towns very close to Sinjar, like Baaj to the south, and the Turkomen city of Tel Afar to the east, became strongholds for the Sunni insurgency. Sinjar became an unwitting pit stop for fighters and weapons coming into Iraq to fuel the mayhem.

In Sinjar, communal peace had been partly maintained through the Yezidis' krief system, where a male Yezidi child is circumcised on the lap of a man from another religion or caste, often a Sunni Arab. It is impossible to convert to Yezidism, and marriage between the three Yezidi castes is strictly prohibited. The krief would then be a godparent to the child, and the families would be tied together in kinship. The system acknowledged both ethnic and religious tensions and tried to mediate a way through them.

"Sinjar was like one house; we were all brothers: the Shia, Yezidis, Christians, and Kurds," said Abdulrahman, thirty, a Sunni Muslim from Sinjar, who has a Kurdish mother and an Arab father. His family had fifteen Yezidi kriefs—all of whom were circumcised on his father's lap. "Our weddings were like their weddings. We celebrated holidays together and if anyone fought with [the Yezidis] the Krief would come and stand at their door and say 'my blood for your blood.'"

As the Kurdish hold on Sinjar grew and the security situation deteriorated, Sunni Arabs visiting from outlying areas had to show their ID cards and in some cases needed a sponsor to enter Sinjar or nearby Yezidi towns. "The Arabs from Bleej hated the Kurds from Sinjar because when they wanted to go into Sinjar, the Peshmerga made it really hard and were searching them," said Abdulrahman, who grew up in Sinjar city and fled to Mosul after ISIS took control.

His mother, Aisha, forty-five, a Kurdish Muslim, said that under Peshmerga control Sinjar was safer. They were strict but acted "with respect," she said, blaming any problems on the Arabs from outlying towns such as Baaj and Bleej, which were known as hotspots of extremism.

Sunni Muslims living in Sinjar were mostly middle-class traders and in conversations they distanced themselves from the tragedy that followed and blamed the rise of ISIS in the area on the rural Muslim population who belonged to a lower socioeconomic class.

Sunnis in Iraq are not homogeneous or politically unified and not all Sunnis rejected the post-2003 order. They are not the only group dissatisfied with the "new Iraq": recent years have seen large-scale Shia protests at poor governance and stifled opportunity.

As security tightened and attacks increased, the Yezidis stopped visiting their Arab kriefs as often, and the tradition waned. Local disputes had been mostly between tribes, but in the violent post-2003 world, sectarian and ethnic definitions sharpened. Younger generations of Yezidis grew up with less exposure to their Muslim neighbors.

The krief system, and the informal assurance of tribal mediation it gave, began to unravel.

This was part of a wider trend in Iraq. Communities hunkered down, blast walls or new berms went up, and suspicion spread across sectarian and ethnic lines. This peaked in the 2006–7 sectarian civil war, when Sunnis were cleansed from parts of Baghdad by Shia militias in response to Sunni insurgent attacks on Shia holy sites. Violence was pandemic.

In Iraqi Kurdistan, after years of repression, the younger generation grew up learning Kurdish instead of Arabic. The lack of Arabic meant interaction with their fellow Iraqis was more difficult.

This was the situation in 2007 when the bombs struck Sinjar. Afterward, relations between Arabs and Yezidis dramatically worsened as the Peshmerga stepped up security controls at checkpoints around Sinjar.

"Most of the Arabs were living to the south and west," Ali, the Yezidi fighter from Siba Sheikheder, recalled. "They had to come to Siba to redeem their food stamps. The Peshmerga made it hard for them so they avoided coming. Before that, we would go wherever we wanted to visit Arabs for funerals and weddings, and they would come to the town."

New earth berms were erected around Siba Sheikheder. It was at this berm that the men waited uneasily in the early hours of August 3, 2014, armed with light weapons that some of them had kept from their days fighting with the Iraqi army, the Iraqi police, or the Peshmerga.

Some had no experience fighting at all.

--

Zorro Garis, forty, a Yezidi farmer and border policeman, lay sleeping beside his wife in the town of Gerzerik, east of Siba Sheikheder, in those early hours of August 3. When I interviewed him later, his eyes looked tired, perhaps because of his eleven children, or perhaps because of what happened on that summer day in 2014.

He was at home on leave from his job guarding the Saudi–Iraq border. Getting there took seventeen hours by car, and he believes he was posted there because of his unpopularity with his superiors.

A month earlier, ISIS had seized a few farms not far from Gerzerik and began firing at the town. Zorro could see the fighters' cars going back and forth and recognized them as local Arabs.

The men of Gerzerik reinforced the earth berms with sandbags supplied by the Peshmerga, and began taking it in turns to stand guard each night. They were joined in defending the town by a few hundred Peshmerga fighters, mostly Yezidis, along with some Muslim Kurds, and nearly all from the Kurdish PUK party.

In the early hours of August 3, Zorro's wife awoke to a phone call from her nephew who said that a convoy of ISIS cars was approaching. Zorro roused himself from sleep and went out to help.

At the berm, he saw the lights of two cars drawing near, within weapon range. They were heading toward the old part of the town where the Peshmerga were stationed. Zorro watched as the cars stopped and the fighters got out. ISIS shouted to the Peshmerga, telling them to turn themselves in. The Peshmerga began shooting back and managed to destroy the cars.

"And then the war started," said Zorro. It was 2:15 a.m. Four-strong groups of local men were positioned at even intervals along the berm to the south of Gerzerik. The Peshmerga were based on either side, and ISIS was firing mortars into the town. Zorro recalled the sound of women screaming as the mortars landed.

Zorro's wife called to ask him if they should leave. He told her to gather their children in one small room.

"If you are hit by a mortar you will all be killed together and if you're lucky you all will be saved," he said.

By now the mortars were coming down like rain.

Along with three of his neighbors, "Qassim," sixty-one, a builder from Gerzerik, was guarding a different point on the berm. A moustachioed veteran of the 1980s Iran–Iraq war, he describes the fight that night as being "like an American movie."

Around 4 a.m. there was a lull and it seemed that the battle was over.

After a short reprieve, likely so the ISIS soldiers could observe the dawn prayers, the second attack began. This time ISIS had armored cars and bombarded the villagers with machine-gun fire.

Zorro raised his head over the berm and looked around. He saw a young man 150 meters away wearing black and firing mortars toward him. He tried to shoot but struggled to aim his Kalashnikov. He didn't want to shoot on automatic fire and expend all his ammunition, but after several attempts, he managed to hit the young man.

"Two minutes later I raised my head again and saw there were now Humvees just behind the berms. They were driving and shooting at people," Zorro said.

The Humvees were likely seized from the Iraqi army during the ISIS summer blitzkrieg through Mosul and farther south. Only the berm remained between Zorro and ISIS. He shouted for his group of fighters to run for cover.

It was 6:30 a.m., and day was breaking.

--

In Siba Sheikheder, the first mortars came fifteen minutes after the battle in Gerzerik began.

They hit the police station. The Peshmerga returned fire. Next, ISIS convoys attacked from the south and western fronts and the villagers fought back with small arms. At the edge of the town, the Peshmerga fired a heavy machine gun but the ammunition soon ran out.

Ali's house was not far from the police station in the center of town, and at around 4 a.m., when the fighting paused, he rushed home to check on his family. They wanted to leave. He told them to wait, remembering the agreement they had all made to stay and fight.

Throughout the night, the men, including Peshmerga, were constantly calling for backup, but nothing was coming. Between 5:30 and 6 a.m., the Peshmerga abandoned the front line on the west side of Siba Sheikheder.

Ali looked up and saw car lights moving on the Mountain ahead of him. The sun had just risen and by now he could see the cars on the Mountain road. "Finally, backup is arriving," he thought to himself. They were going to win. He later learned these were the cars of families already fleeing Sinjar and rushing to the Mountain for safety.

It was then that Ali and the other fighters saw the familiar dust trail through the desert. It was unmistakable. ISIS trucks heading toward them. Three cars came from the north toward the police station. They took control of it with no resistance and began shooting randomly as the fighters poured out into the streets. ISIS raised their flag on the police station and shouted "Allahu Akbar"—God is greatest.

It was just before 7 a.m.

People began to panic. "Nobody is coming, run for your life," someone shouted at Ali, "try to run. Save yourself." Some fighters tried to go back to fight. Ali, using a ditch to shield himself from the hail of bullets, headed toward the east. He saw bodies falling around him as he ran.

One young man who ran back to fight, called his father an hour later to say he was now surrounded by ISIS. Another man who fought on that day recalled ISIS fighters arriving in two vehicles and surrounding fifty men who were then blindfolded, led away, and shot.

Later I met the daughter of one of the border guards who was kidnapped by ISIS. Three years on, she is now twenty and has a thin, sunken face, and was being treated for panic attacks caused by the memory of her four-year-old sister, Aziza, dying from a bullet wound as the family ran from ISIS in Siba Sheikheder.

"Where is Aziza?" she asked the doctor, in a state of confusion. The doctor leaned forward and asked her about her relationship with her brothers and sisters before the war. Her breathing continued to rise in nervous waves.

"Where do you feel pain?" he asked her.

"I can't breathe," she replied, panting. "I have a headache and I'm losing my mind."

He asked her if she was going to school. "No," she answered.

"She hasn't eaten since yesterday," her father added.

Back in the camp, she was drowsy but still fighting back waves of anxiety. Her eyes fluttered shut.

At the moment when her sister had died, thousands of villagers were rushing to break down the earth berms so they could escape faster. The road was crammed with cars and people walking and running, trying to leave as the bullets kept flying.

Ali headed for his ancestral village at the foothills of the Mountain. To get there he had to cross the highway linking Mosul to the Syrian city of Raqqa, also under ISIS control. He passed a convoy of Peshmerga fighters heading north around the Mountain. It was nearly 8 a.m.

ISIS had taken the Yezidi villages south of Sinjar, and the other towns would soon fall like dominoes. Ali wanted to go back to Siba Sheikheder to collect his things, but it was too late.

He watched with others as a convoy of ISIS fighters headed east toward Sinjar itself.

--

In Gerzerik, villagers were also abandoning defenses and running from the front line. As Zorro ran, his brother and two cousins were shot and killed. He went home and found his house deserted. His wife had taken the car and fled. He joined his neighbors and drove away from the town.

Qassim fled from the berm at the same time, when he saw an armored ISIS vehicle approaching. "We didn't have weapons to destroy it—we were out of ammunition so we had to run," he recalled.

Three of the village men were killed by sniper and machine-gun fire. In the center of town Qassim saw the bodies of those killed by mortars, and two cars full of Peshmerga fighters.

They were the last to leave.

"We fought for six hours and nobody came. . . . The Peshmerga were fighting side by side with us but they did not get support . . . my son was with a Peshmerga unit. One of them was a sniper; he was a very brave man and he fought until his last breath," Qassim said.

One Peshmerga fighter smashed his phone on the ground in frustration after calling his leaders repeatedly for backup and receiving no response. Jidaan Darush, from Tel Banat, who is now a Peshmerga deputy commander under KDP command, recalled trying to call in artillery to hit ISIS positions two kilometers away, but the artillery unit had already left.

"I have been in many battles and wars," Qassim said sadly, "when a betrayal starts happening I know. When you don't get backup and support it means something is going on." Qassim believes the Peshmerga were instructed to withdraw earlier that morning but those stationed in Gerzerik disobeyed the order and stayed on to fight. Three of them died.

"Militarily the area had technically fallen and any force that stayed there would have been massacred," said Halo Penjweni, a member of the PUK leadership council. He estimated the number of Peshmerga in the area as around ten thousand, mostly from the KDP. The real number was likely far lower taking into account shift patterns, generous leave allocations, and the Peshmerga's own ghost soldier problem, leaving small groups of Peshmerga on duty, spread out thinly at small checkpoints.[32]

At 7 a.m., Zorro fled along the dirt roads to avoid ISIS, who were still shooting. He was desperately thirsty and begged his friends to stop at a nearby farmhouse and take some bottles of water.

Qassim saw people streaming from towns near Sinjar on foot, in cars, tractors, and with their flocks of sheep—a panicked current of people and animals surging north as daylight came.

The resistance the local men put up against ISIS may have been limited and in the end defeated, but it bought valuable time for others to escape and undoubtedly saved many lives.

News of the battle was spreading to the men and women in other towns and villages around the Mountain. An estimated 9,900 Yezidis were killed or kidnapped over the following days, but those that did survive owe a great deal to these men, many of whom were not professional fighters and died out on the berms so that others could live.[33]

As Qassim fled Gerzerik, women at the roadside thrust two young babies into his arms so that they could be taken to the Mountain. After an anxious wait, he found the women again and reunited the mother with her small children.

When he described this to me a year and a half later outside his partially built home, 130 miles from Sinjar, his voice became choked with emotion and his eyes grew moist. He fell suddenly silent, alone with his memories.

Chapter 3

"They were killing our men in the valley"

"They could not fight so they retreated," said Major General Aziz Waisi, the head of the Zerevani, a well-equipped, mostly infantry force aligned with the KDP. He denied that his men were given an order to retreat. "Some of them fought until the last bullet and the roads were closed." After that they withdrew and reorganized, he said.

"It was an exceptional situation no military force could [stand]. The fighting was unbalanced and out of our control." ISIS attacked quickly from every direction, which is why the withdrawal wasn't communicated to the Yezidis, he said.

There were around seven hundred Zerevani on active duty in Sinjar on August 2, 2014, he told me, adding that he wasn't in direct command of them. "We believed we could defeat them and we wanted people to stay because it was not our decision to leave Shingal [Sinjar]. In the military no one is always successful—sometimes they are defeated."

The circumstances surrounding the Peshmergas' retreat from Sinjar have become a subject of severe controversy. KDP officials insist that they stayed and fought, while Yezidis say they were abandoned. These competing narratives are today fueling new tensions in Sinjar and preventing the city's rehabilitation.

"Many of our forces were mortared, killed, captured but we didn't have the reinforcements to send. . . . It was very hard at the beginning: it was a new fight . . . ISIS had a lot of equipment from the Iraqi army," he explained in his office in Erbil, at the Zerevani headquarters.

Men like Waisi, Peshmerga who fought Saddam's army from Kurdistan's Mountains, were not used to the ISIS style of warfare, which combined insurgent tactics with sleeper cells and ground offensives. Younger Peshmerga had done little more than man checkpoints.

Before ISIS attacked Kurdistan in August 2014, the Peshmerga moved to control parts of the disputed territories across northern Iraq, such as Kirkuk and its surrounding oil infrastructure, south of the regional capital, Erbil. This move coincided with a vacuum created when the Iraqi security fled. President of the Kurdistan Region and leader of the KDP Masoud Barzani said a referendum on Kurdish independence from Iraq would be held in a matter of months. The Kurds have long dreamed of declaring independence from Iraq. The goal seemed to be in reach during the summer of 2014: the relationship between Erbil and the central government had eroded in recent years, and now Baghdad was fighting against the collapse of Iraq. The Peshmerga fanned out along the new front line with ISIS, but like the Peshmerga itself, the new front was split between KDP and PUK command.

"The Peshmerga blocked ISIS in some places even though the Kurds were lightly armed, whilst in other places similarly equipped Kurdish units retreated. The primary difference was leadership, not weapons," said Michael Knights.

The "inability or unwillingness to share evidence" between the intelligence services of the different Kurdish parties was also seen to be a factor in the Fall of Sinjar, according to the International Crisis Group.[34]

--

In the early hours of the morning of the attack, "Manjie," forty, was anxiously talking on her phone to relatives in Gerzerik while her six children slept. Her husband had just gone up to the roof of their home in Sinjar city to listen to the distant rumble of incoming fire. The warm night air brought out clouds of mosquitoes that had to be batted away.

That morning Manjie made breakfast with tomatoes and cucumbers brought over by a neighbor. After they'd eaten,

Manjie went outside and was surprised to see the same neighbor hastily packing their car. Her Shia neighbors were also preparing to run, leaving behind an elderly uncle to watch over the house.

Manjie and her family didn't have a car, but decided they, too, should leave. They set off from the house, walking toward the Mountain. There were twenty-one of them altogether, including Manjie's husband, his two wives, and their children. Manjie's eldest daughter was already married and escaped by car with her husband's family from Gerzerik.

The rapid advance of ISIS and the withdrawal of the Peshmerga broadly meant that those who had cars managed to escape, and those who didn't were captured. It was poorer families who were the most vulnerable as they fled, and many women in these families were illiterate, which would later make escaping from captivity even harder.

"Nergez," a warm-hearted thirty-five-year-old mother of five, was sleeping on the roof of her home in Tel Banat, southeast of Sinjar city, a common way to keep cool in the scorching Iraqi summer. She was woken by gunshots and what sounded like bullets hitting the walls of the house.

At daybreak, Nergez and her family tried to flee on foot, but were turned back by the Peshmerga and told to defend the town. "If they had let us go no one would have been caught," said her niece, who sat beside Nergez as she talked. Her husband was a day laborer but is now a Peshmerga fighter. He appeared to be in shock, and let

Nergez do the talking. From the tears that occasionally glistened in his eyes, however, it was clear he was listening to our conversation.

When they saw that the Peshmerga had left, they ran from the town now with no one to stop them. They traveled on foot for fourteen kilometers, avoiding the highway that had already been seized by ISIS. By then it was brutally hot, and the plains of Sinjar were orange and yellow, burnt dry by the sun. Above them the tall crags of the Mountain rose in the distance.

Hundreds of other Yezidis were fleeing in the same direction in confusion and panic. The elderly, ill, and young were struggling to walk. "We didn't know how to go to the Mountain and we weren't sure about the roads," Nergez told me. They tried to find shelter in the undulating hills, corraled together like sheep, looking up fearfully at airplanes in the blue sky above.

--

Manjie and her children were scrambling up the winding road that leads to the Mountain when gunshots broke out. They scattered, running, but then she stopped and panicked. Where was her husband? They could still hear gunfire but the road was blocked with people and traffic.

"Let's go back. What are we going to do? They've killed our men," she asked.

"You can't go back," the people around her said, "they're killing the men and taking the women."

"We have to go back to our men," she decided. It was 10 a.m.

Meanwhile, Manjie's husband had been captured and moved to an abandoned building in the city. Here, one of the prisoners tried to argue with an ISIS guard who responded by slapping. At the crack of the fighter's hand on the man, Manjie's husband knew they would be killed. The ISIS guards were talking among themselves about what they would do when the other fighters arrived. When the guards went to pray, Manjie's husband took the opportunity to flee. As he ran, Manjie and her children came back to look for him. They were captured.

Across town, Kne Qassim, a fifty-seven-year-old woman from a town south of Sinjar, was cowering, being forcibly held at a chicken farm. Her husband, son, and dozens of other Yezidi men were led away to a patch of scrubland nearby.

"They put us inside and we heard gunshots," she told me later. "They were killing our men in the valley."

--

Inside Sinjar's main hospital, a yellow, two-story building near the KDP headquarters, Sabah, a thirty-year-old nurse, lay sleeping. He was on the night shift, and the sun was yet to rise when one of his colleagues shook him. "Wake up," he heard as he struggled out of sleep, "Sinjar is under attack by Daesh [ISIS]."

At 6 a.m. the first injured people arrived from Gerzerik; and then for the next two hours, thirty to forty injured Yezidi civilians and fighters poured from towns to the south. Most were suffering from gunshots and mortar injuries. He also remembers seeing injured Yezidis from the Asayish force (the Kurdish intelligence).

"Suddenly I heard gunfire near the hospital," he recalled. "I went outside by the gate and saw two local gunmen." They were wearing civilian clothes and were guarding the entrance to the hospital. Two Peshmerga fighters came out of the KDP branch headquarters and Sabah watched as the gunmen confiscated their weapons before letting them go.

Sabah wasn't that alarmed. He thought perhaps the gunmen would eventually leave, so he went back inside to treat his injured patients. It wasn't until a little while later that he realized he might be in danger. One of the guards came inside and told the doctors that they were no longer allowed to treat any Yezidis or Peshmergas. Feeling that something wasn't right, Sabah went to a side room and began to change out of his hospital clothes in preparation to leave.

Meanwhile the group of ISIS fighters outside the hospital was growing in number. Inside, the doctors were about to treat a Yezidi fighter from Gerzerik who was in critical condition, but were under pressure from the men outside not to. The doctor asked his assistant, Muhanad, an Arab from the Mutaywit tribe, to go and find out if this was true.

When he came back, Muhanad confirmed that the order was in fact correct and he told the patient to leave. Sabah and

Muhanad slept in the same room in the hospital. When they weren't working, they used to hang out, drinking tea and watching TV together. Sabah considered him a friend.

"Daesh [ISIS] wants you to go outside," Muhanad told him.

It was a little before 9 a.m. Outside, Sabah found himself standing in front of a bearded Iraqi man wearing a long tunic. "He put a gun in my back and said 'move,'" Sabah said. He pushed Sabah toward a Toyota pickup parked at the hospital's gate with about half a dozen fighters in it, all of them dressed in a similar fashion. He remembers crowds of civilians gathering around the fighters.

"They asked me if I was a Yezidi. I said 'Yes, but I'm doing a humanitarian job and I've never carried a weapon.'"

"You are a Yezidi, so you have to shut up and get in the car," the man responded.

The ISIS fighter ordered Muhanad to go inside and bring out any Yezidis who were accompanying the wounded. He came back with four men who were also interrogated. They were now surrounded by dozens of ISIS fighters in cars and trucks. Some were waving ISIS flags. Locals were just walking beside them, cheering and jostling with their guns held aloft. Sabah was shepherded into a car full of gun-toting fighters, and was driven through the center of town, toward the bazaar in Sinjar's old town.

"Every once in a while they would stop and talk to other Daesh fighters on the way. When we passed by the market I saw more cars driving back and forth," Sabah said. The ISIS fighters were in civilian cars with heavy machine guns. "They shouldn't have been able to take the city but they did." At the eastern junction on the Mosul–Raqqa highway, he saw ISIS fighters coming in "from all sides, fifteen of their cars were parked there."

Sabah was taken to Tel Qasab, southeast of Sinjar, where he was threatened and told to convert to Islam. He was almost killed, until a local ISIS official, Abu Hamza al-Khawatina, arrived and set him free. Abu Hamza would later be identified by survivors as the fighter in charge of negotiating with the village elders of Kojo in the weeks before they were massacred. Sabah went to his home in Tel Banat and hid for five days before escaping to the Mountain with the help of his Arab friends.

People woke up on that morning to find that Sinjar had changed hands and was now under ISIS control. It had fallen with barely a shot being fired, taken by a surprisingly small number of fighters. As in other ISIS battles, the power of the group didn't lie in its military strength, but in the disorganization and poor leadership of its enemies.

The man who commanded the attack on Sinjar, according to Hisham al-Hashimi, an adviser to the Iraqi government on ISIS, was Abu Muslim al-Turkmani, a long-time jihadist and former officer in the Iraqi army. Turkmani's real name was Fadil al-Hayali and he was an aide to ISIS leader Abu Bakr al-Baghdadi. Like many ISIS leaders, after the 2003 invasion he spent time in Camp Bucca, a US-run prison in southern Iraq.

When Turkmani was subsequently killed in a US strike on August 18, 2015, near Mosul, the White House described him as a "primary coordinator for moving large amounts of weapons, explosives, vehicles, and people between Iraq and Syria."[35]

Contrary to the imagery at the time, ISIS was not an external force sweeping across the desert border between Iraq and Syria. Rather, it had ties with several Sunni Arab jihadist and Baathist militant groups before its successful seizure of Mosul.

ISIS reportedly seized Mosul with the assistance of other Sunni insurgent groups. An anonymous KDP official claimed that the party was in dialogue with these insurgents, enabling a tacit, although eventually temporary, cease-fire along the northern Peshmerga lines.[36] After Mosul fell, ISIS moved to consolidate control and crush its former insurgent allies, at which point it also began attacking KRG-controlled areas like Sinjar.[37] This theory, although unproven, could explain the ill-preparedness of Kurdish forces to defend the area, allowing Sinjar to fall in near silence.

When the offensive began against Sinjar and other Arab-Kurd disputed areas, it was Nineveh's ethnic and religious minorities who found themselves on the first line of defense and became the primary victims of the Peshmerga's withdrawal as ISIS then advanced toward the Kurdistan region's capital, Erbil.

Sinjar fell in a single morning, but the factors that allowed it to fall were a long time in the making.

On that morning, Abdulrahman, a Sunni Muslim, went to work as usual in his car mechanics shop in the market near Sinjar's old town. The market was closed and he saw Yezidis fleeing toward the Mountain using whatever they could to carry their belongings. Shortly after 7 a.m., he saw a small number of fighters driving through the market in half a dozen pickup trucks and a few cars, but no actual fighting.

"It was all quiet and then, every once in a while, we could hear gunshots," said Thama, who was still in the city. "Most people were too scared to leave their homes," he said. ISIS fighters went quickly to blow up Sinjar's Shia Zeynab shrine, which was near Abdulrahman's house. They then began breaking into and stealing from the houses of Shia Muslims.

The next day, families that remained tried to shield their children from the sight of Yezidi corpses lying in the roads. The Sunni Muslims looked on in fear at their new rulers now that the Shia, Christians, and Yezidis had all gone. They had seen scores of women being trucked away to Tel Afar and they didn't know what would happen to them.

They got their answer a few days later when ISIS called for former Iraqi policemen to gather at the mosque and offer their public repentance to the militants. Abdulrahman's father obeyed and went to the mosque with hundreds of other men. They were still there days later when what they say was an air strike hit the Rahman mosque, killing dozens of them.[38] Body parts littered the floor, traumatized survivors later told me. Sunni families decided it wasn't safe to stay and many fled to Mosul or other parts of the caliphate. When they left, ISIS seized their homes and belongings.

--

In the aftermath of Sinjar falling to ISIS, Baba Sheikh, the Yezidi religious leader who holds a position similar to that of the pope for Catholics, remembered meeting President Barzani.

"Please, I beg you . . . our sins . . . tell me what happened. Was it a betrayal? Was it carelessness?" he asked Barzani, breaking down in tears.

Senior KRG and Peshmerga officials express remorse and regret over the fall of Sinjar, but continue to define the Yezidis as ethnically Kurdish and therefore Sinjar as a natural part of the KRG, even while many Yezidis from Sinjar disavow Kurdish ethnicity in the wake of the ISIS attack.

"I understand some Yezidis have been hurt," Fuad Hussein, Barzani's chief of staff, told me later, adding that the Peshmerga morale was low after the defeat in Zummar, which happened in the days before. "If I was Yezidi I would not trust any human being because [. . .] If I saw a man killing my daughter, attacking us or taking my mother, this is a normal reaction. But politically, socially, geographically, strategically, in the end Yezidis are Kurds. Linguistically their future is interlinked with the other Kurds. This is a reality."

Less than a week after the fall of Sinjar on August 3, 2014, ISIS advanced toward Erbil.

On the evening of Thursday, August 7, President Barack Obama, who had campaigned on a promise to draw down the wars in Iraq and Afghanistan, stood at a podium in the White House and talked about the Yezidis:

"Today I authorized two operations in Iraq—targeted air strikes to protect our American personnel, and a humanitarian effort to help save thousands of Iraqi civilians who are trapped on a mountain without food and water and facing almost certain death."

Six days after Sinjar fell to ISIS, US fighter jets dropped two five-hundred-pound laser-guided bombs on ISIS artillery that was pointing directly at the Kurdish city of Erbil (home to a US consulate), and dropped food and water to the Yezidis stranded on the Mountain.[39]

But in the days before the US strikes began, Syrian Kurdish guerrilla fighters had already crossed the border and began gouging a safe corridor through ISIS-held territory, between Syria and the north side of the Mountain, rescuing tens of thousands of Yezidis trapped on the Mountain, and bringing them back to Iraqi Kurdistan via their emerging statelet in northern Syria.

--

"Zerif," a former KDP employee from northern Sinjar, is in her late twenties and gives an impression of fearlessness. She has a deep laugh and sparkling green eyes. Throughout the night of August 2, she was in touch with the KDP central office in Sinjar, and at 5 a.m. she remembers a Peshmerga fighter telling her:

"We've left everything behind. If you can, take your family and try to escape." Staff at her local KDP branch had told her she should stay. "I owe [that Peshmerga] something because he was telling me the truth," she said.

When the villagers awoke, the Peshmerga had already gone or were in the process of leaving. At 10:30 a.m., her family were still undecided about what to do, but her friend, the Muslim Peshmerga, phoned again and told her that ISIS had already reached Hardan in the east and were heading toward her town.

Half an hour later, cars riddled with bullet holes and full of injured and terrified people fleeing from the south side of the Mountain began arriving. Her family decided to escape, but the road was by now so crowded that it was hard to make progress. When Zerif saw vehicles filled with Peshmerga fighters driving alongside them, she rolled down her window and shouted:

"Why aren't you fighting?"

"We have no weapons or ammunition," came the response. "We have nothing." The men that were supposed to protect them were also trying to escape.

The road north ran along the Syrian border and was surrounded by flat wide plains, dotted with Arab farms and villages. Some of these villages were already out of government control and Zerif thought that it would only take one "kid carrying a gun" and they would all be dead. But now, with growing knowledge about the killings to the south, they had no choice but to carry on.

As they drove north toward the Kurdistan region, they came to the town of Rabia, where Zerif saw ISIS fighters in cars by the sides of the road. The Yezidis were crammed into trucks and large family cars. They collided with other cars as they tried to drive away. "There were cars with dead and injured people inside. We didn't know what would happen to us but we were still driving; women and children were crying."

Rabia is the home of the powerful Arab Shammar tribal confederation. In years gone by, the tribesmen employed the Yezidis as laborers on their vegetable farms. Zerif worked on the Shammar farms in Rabia tending tomatoes and cucumbers with her family when she was younger. Drought, poverty, and a lack of jobs forced many Yezidi families to do the same. Today you can still see the mud huts where Yezidi farmhands lived.

On the way into Rabia, the fleeing convoy came to a standstill. To the west was the Syrian border and to the east was a large expanse of fields and villages stretching toward ISIS-held Mosul. From this direction, ISIS fighters were firing mortars and bullets at the logjam of civilian cars.

"We were all terrified and crying; but then we saw a military car coming from the Syrian side. There were five women fighters in that car. We didn't know who they were and we thought they were ISIS. Two of them helped the cars to move and the other three gathered the Peshmergas' weapons and fired back toward ISIS, which allowed the traffic to move."

These new strangers told the Yezidis to run for their lives.

Chapter 4

"There was almost no life but you could see people moving"

The fighters Zerif saw that day were from Rojava, an enclave of northeastern Syria carved out by Syrian Kurds who had been persecuted and denied basic rights. In the power vacuum following the start of Syria's civil war, fighters from the Kurdish People's Protection Units (YPG)—the Syrian affiliate of the PKK (Kurdistan Worker's Party)—battled ISIS to stake out their territory.

The PKK was founded by Abdullah Öcalan in Turkey in the late 1970s as a Marxist, Kurdish separatist organization. In 1984, the group took up arms against the Turkish state for Kurdish rights and freedoms. The PKK used terror tactics like suicide bombings, and guerrilla attacks against the Turkish army, Kurdish opponent groups, and even their own members who were accused of treachery.[40]

Turkish reprisals against the PKK's attacks led to war in the southeast of Turkey. Hundreds of villages were destroyed and more than thirty thousand were killed on both sides. The PKK is on the terror list in the US, the EU, and Turkey, and the group maintains bases in the mountains where the borders of Turkey, Iran, and Iraq converge; and smuggling is rife.

In 1999, Öcalan was arrested in Nairobi, Kenya and is now serving a life sentence in a prison off the coast of Istanbul. Since his imprisonment, the war has continued in fits and starts. A wealth of civil society groups, many of which support the PKK to some degree, have sprung up pursuing rights for Turkey's fifteen million Kurds. A cease-fire between the Turkish government and the PKK, brokered in 2013, ended in July 2015, in part because of the overspill from the war in Syria.

In prison, Öcalan's views began to change. He moved away from the Marxism of his youth and embraced a political philosophy emphasizing localized power over that of the nation-state. The PKK distanced itself from the idea of Kurdish separatism and these new ideas informed how the three cantons in Rojava, northern Syria would be run.[41] The governing authorities of Rojava, despite high-minded goals, have also been accused of silencing opponents through arbitrary arrests, harassment, and abuses in detention.[42]

The PKK has long had a presence in Sinjar, which is strategically important as a land route into Rojava. In 2006, Turkish officials complained to the US Ambassador to Turkey about the presence of PKK front offices in Iraq, including in Sinjar.[43]

PKK ideology continues to have potency among Iraqi Kurdish youth, aided by their political party offices, which are decorated with images of Öcalan. Many Iraqi Kurds have gone to join the PKK as guerrilla fighters in the mountains, but the group is still viewed with suspicion. The PKK fought the KDP in the intra-Kurdish civil war of the 1990s and has since maintained frosty relations with the Iraqi Kurdish ruling party, while enjoying better relations with the PUK.[44]

When the war with ISIS began, the PKK came down from their mountain camps to help the Peshmerga push the jihadists back from the borders of Iraqi Kurdistan, including in the KDP-dominated Makhmour district in Erbil province. This, along with the YPG's successes against ISIS in Syria (particularly in Kobane), gave the group new international cachet, despite criticism of some of its practices, such as the recruitment of child soldiers.[45]

--

It was not only the Kurds in Rojava who took advantage of the bloodshed in Syria; the jihadists of Al-Qaeda in Iraq moved across the border after the Sunni tribes in Anbar turned against them with US backing. The smuggling operations along the border switched and instead of bringing fighters and weapons into Iraq, they went the other way to Syria where President Bashar al-Assad had brutally put down protests against him that had begun as part of the Arab Spring.[46]

A Yezidi writer from Sinjar, "Haskan," remembers smugglers on the border hiding weapons in local farms before moving them across to Syria. Sometimes the farms were raided by the border police and the smugglers were caught, but more often than not, they could bribe their way out. During the Syrian war in 2012 and 2013, jihadists became more powerful, eventually moving to directly control large areas of territory.[47]

"You had to be part of it; otherwise the militias wouldn't let you smuggle," said Haskan, recalling the growing ties between his Sunni Arab krief's family from the Khawatina tribe, who were smugglers, and the jihadists in Syria. Under sanctions against Iraq in the 1990s, smugglers traded oil, livestock, and cigarettes, but the war economy in Syria's shifted the trade to more lucrative items.

--

The Americans had been paying the Sunni tribes fighting extremists in their own communities, but when the responsibility for tribal support shifted back to the government in Baghdad, the project was threatened because Sunnis still remained on the periphery of national politics.[48]

After elections in 2010, Sunnis had a chance to gain representation when Iyad Allawi, a secular Shia Muslim, nearly became prime minister; but instead Maliki hung on and began consolidating power, particularly in the security ministries.[49]

The last US troops pulled out of Iraq at the end of 2011 after a period of eight years at war in which at least 120,000 Iraqis were killed (although the real number is probably far higher). 4,802 US and coalition troops lost their lives, and an estimated 1.5 million Iraqis were internally displaced.[50] Tens of thousands also fled abroad, mainly to neighboring countries.

As Maliki's strength grew, Sunni power was divided between leaders who remained close to the Prime Minister, and those who felt increasingly marginalized by widespread arrests under the guise of fighting terrorism, and de-Baathification.[51]

In December 2012, security forces arrested the guards and staff members of Iraqi finance minister and prominent Sunni, Rafea al-Issawi, on charges of terrorism, forcing Issawi to flee to exile. Peaceful protests in his hometown of Fallujah followed, and, emboldened by the protests in Syria, they quickly spread to Hawija in Kirkuk province and to the Anbari provincial capital of Ramadi and other Sunni-majority areas.

The Sunni anti-government protests grew, made up of local organizations as well as tribes, clerics, politicians, activists, and former resistance fighters.[52] The demands of the protesters went from the release of Issawi's guards and of female prisoners, to the cancellation of the Anti-Terrorism law, the rollback of de-Baathification measures, and a more equitable sectarian balance in Iraqi state institutions.[53] The protests rejected the legitimacy of the Baghdad government, and included sectarian, anti-Shia rhetoric. Baath-era flags were flown, and concern grew in Baghdad that the protests were being infiltrated with extremists and insurgent groups.

Clashes began occurring at the protests. In April 2013, security forces stormed a protest camp in Hawija, Kirkuk province. Fifty people were killed and ten injured. This began another descent into sectarian violence and the monthly civilian death toll spiked.

As the political situation in Iraq deteriorated, extremists became bolder. Insurgents succeeded in launching a series of large-scale prison breaks, and carrying out a virulent campaign of assassination against moderate Sunni community leaders, opponents, and security officials.

In late 2013, I met a teacher working in Mosul who described how jihadists were able to extort money for protection from businesses and contractors in the city and kill those who didn't pay, revealing how they were already well entrenched in the city's corruption networks. Kidnappings, assassinations, threats, and other attacks were common. He began to modify his lessons and made sure he didn't say anything against ISIS, in case they had spies among his students.

Government forces were massing near the Sunni anti-government protest sites in Fallujah and Ramadi at the end of

2013 and tribal fighters were also gathering. In Ramadi, Iraqi forces negotiated a withdrawal but ISIS fighters seized the moment to enter and ransack police stations.[54] Clashes at the edge of Fallujah ended in an Iraqi siege, while ISIS took over the center.[55]

By the start of 2014, Fallujah, known as the city of mosques, had fallen to ISIS. "From January 3 onwards, ISIL patrols cruised Fallujah city in captured police vehicles using megaphones to call policemen to repent."[56] Ramadi remained in government control but under attack until the spring of the following year when an emboldened ISIS eliminated the remaining pockets of resistance.

In Sinjar, the militants across the border were growing in power. "In my krief's family, the younger guys joined ISIS," Haskan said. "The older men in the family refused to join. They even called my father and told him to run away, but the younger members of the family joined [ISIS] because they had these years of business relationships with them."

Many insurgents in Iraq came from local communities and were paid to carry out acts of violence. A police officer in Kirkuk in October 2012 explained that a person would be paid $50 to plant a bomb. "The group drops the bomb off in a bag with $50 in an envelope. A random executioner, recruited for the occasion, picks the bag up and places the explosive at the desired spot."[57]

A resident of the border city of Al-Qa'im in Anbar province described the fall of his city and how ISIS capitalized on grievances with the government and the Sunni protest movement:

"Fifteen fighters entered the city. During Friday prayers they announced they had come to end government injustices and terminate the amnesty that police and soldiers enjoyed in the city. Young boys took to the streets cheering victory. The jihadists recruited a number of these who had no connection to the insurgency and no affiliation with political parties but were supporters of the protests. They tasked them with ensuring protection of public and private property, without asking them to swear allegiance. Only after a few weeks of testing their potential were the youths asked to pledge absolute allegiance to Daesh [ISIS]."[58]

In Iraq, the Yezidis were used as a scapegoat by ISIS who capitalized on Sunni outrage over years of perceived injustices and offered a mode of revenge. Yezidi women would become doubly victimized, as women in a male-dominated society, and as part of a religious minority.

ISIS fighters are generally younger, in their early twenties, compared to fighters from Al-Qaeda, who tended to be slightly older, said an anonymous UN political worker. "Iraqis in their forties are not going to join ISIS. The youth are frustrated and see no promises for the future. They are surrounded by corruption and violence and ISIS offers an outlet to push the limits of what can be envisaged as violence. ISIS dehumanizes outsiders. Al-Qaeda did engage—but ISIS failed to interact with anyone."

Now, Zaku, the town of Haskan's krief, is empty except for the occasional visiting guerrilla. The ID cards of the krief's sons were found among the bodies of dead ISIS fighters after a battle with Kurdish militants nearby. "They were my age," he said. "If we had had the relationship we had before 2003 then we would definitely have known them and they would be friends with us—and maybe when ISIS came they wouldn't have harmed the Yezidis."

--

In early July 2014, after the fall of Mosul, PKK leaders in Qandil sent a small group of guerrillas to scope out Sinjar. The guerrillas traveled in secret, wearing civilian clothes because of their ideological rivalry with the ruling KDP in Iraqi Kurdistan.

One of these guerrillas was Dilshir Hakoon. A tall, lanky man with large ears and a heavy brow, he is now a PKK commander in Sinjar. After the fall of Mosul, his group smuggled weapons from Rojava into Sinjar, and young Yezidis out to Rojava for military training.

Like ISIS, PKK's ideology is spread through the indoctrination of recruits. Both organizations emphasize the glory of martyrdom. This makes them well suited enemies although their causes are very different. ISIS follows an extremist version of

Sunni Islam, advocates harsh punishments and the complete lack of freedom for women, while the PKK fights for a radical leftist agenda, including Kurdish rights and the equality of women.

It is likely that ISIS seeded itself in Sinjar with sleeper cells and informants in the communities before they attacked the city, just as the PKK were trying to do—but a fertile groundswell of Sunni Arab resentment meant that ISIS was more successful. The new PKK fighters didn't know the area and didn't yet have the trust of the locals. Their ideology is secular and radically different from Yezidi faith and culture.

After dawn on August 3, when the Peshmerga started to withdraw, the PKK went to retrieve their weapons. But they were too late. Sinjar had already fallen. The guerrillas were trapped and forced to pull back.

At 11 a.m., a group of guerrillas went to the police station in Snuny on the north side of the Mountain and were approached by a group of men who they thought were Yezidis. They had beards and were wearing loose tunics with belts that sported guns and ammunition. They were speaking Arabic. "Other guys said they were ISIS but I didn't believe them," said Dilshir, "I told them 'come.' When I went toward them I thought they are Shangali [Sinjari] people that we could bring with us to fight together."

But drawing closer he realized they were trying to tell the guerrillas to surrender or be killed. There was a firefight and a bigger ISIS force arrived with armored vehicles. The guerrillas retreated to Syria with one of them injured by an ISIS sniper bullet.

--

When the road to Kurdistan became inaccessible due to fighting near Rabia, approximately 130,000 people were stranded on Sinjar Mountain.[59]

For the Yezidis, the world was at first blind to what was happening. People on the Mountain who still had phone signal and battery began desperately calling friends to find out if they were alive; calling for help, protection, food, and water.

Local Yezidis had to defend themselves on the Mountain just as they had tried to do in Gerzerik and Siba Sheikheder. They guarded the main pathways into the foothills where tens of thousands of people were now trapped without food, water, and shelter under the burning sun. A Russian Dushka machine gun was placed at the top of the curved road leading down to Sinjar to fend off ISIS, who were pushing deeper into the valleys of the Mountain, blowing up Yezidi temples along the way.

Through generations of resistance, survival, and storytelling, the Yezidi fighters knew the hills, slopes, and valleys.

The PKK, and their sister group the YPG in Syria, began plotting a route through the desert to free the trapped people on the Mountain. The YPG were already positioned along the border, where they had been fighting to protect the autonomous cantons of Rojava. From there, they needed to push southeast across the plains to the Mountain's north side.

A Yezidi fighter, who is now a commander with a local PKK force, met with the YPG on August 3. The next day, he brought a group of about twenty YPG fighters from the Syrian border to the Mountain, showing them how to thread their way between ISIS positions in the desert carefully. The next day they tried to push ISIS back from the Mountain but were overpowered and had to call in backup from Syria. On August 6, the YPG tried again and managed to force ISIS to retreat from the town of Degury, and then carve a narrow, twenty kilometer pathway to the Syrian border.

ISIS still held the towns and manned positions on each side of the corridor, but they were short of manpower and were not familiar with the area, the local fighter told me. "We were sneaking up to their places and killing them so they were afraid and ran away," he said.

By August 9—a day after the US air strikes began—the corridor was deemed safe enough by most Yezidis, although descending the Mountain on foot, in the heat, was incredibly difficult for the sick, elderly, and families with small children. Dozens of YPG fighters, including their leaders, were killed defending the corridor.

Over the next fifteen days, most of the Yezidis on the Mountain managed to escape across the desert to Syria, under the guard of the YPG.

--

Every few miles along the corridor there was a point manned by guerrillas. Sandstorms whipped around the desert covering faces and vehicles with fine-grained dust that made it impossible to see who was coming toward you: enemy or friend. ISIS attacked their positions with mortars, forcing convoys of civilians back and killing dozens of fighters. Mounds of earth that provided defenses for these positions can still be seen near the Syrian border, years later.

Trucks crowded with people battled through the sandstorm. The fear and the heat were immense, but the guerrillas kept guard, checking the horizon for threat of attack, said a journalist who passed by.[60] The pathway they carved through the desert was littered with abandoned clothing and burnt-out cars that hadn't made it. Flocks of sheep scattered and then disappeared, invisible in the storms of dust.

"We were among seventy people packed into the same truck and I thought my daughter had died because of the heat and thirst. She was on my lap so I covered her with a blanket to keep her cool and to keep the dust inside the truck away from her," said Ahmed Naif, twenty-nine, the only surviving adult male from his family, who were massacred by ISIS near Tel Azer.

At each point, bereft Yezidis stopped and waited to make sure the next stage of the journey was safe. They strained their eyes into the distance to see if an approaching car was filled with ISIS fighters, and felt relieved when they saw the men and the women of the YPG. A Yezidi boy whose family had been killed was given a Kalashnikov and told to stand guard.

In the town of Degury, north of the Mountain, young YPG fighters camped in abandoned buildings and consumed knockoff cola and sugary cakes. From there they could see ISIS-held Snuny, one kilometer away.

--

"Sema Kuchor" is a female guerrilla with the PKK. She has a drawn, elfin-like face, which today is solemn. She arrived in Sinjar on August 5 from Qandil, with forty other female guerrillas who came in response to the attack.

"We started setting up small lookout posts every two or three miles and then we would stay there. When ISIS attacked we would fight them back . . . by the time I arrived the corridor was already open but my job was to protect these positions . . . we wouldn't leave, we would rest where we were; we would eat there and ISIS would be close by. It was like our home.

"Things that you wouldn't imagine in life would be happening on that corridor. There was almost no life but you could see people moving. People would fall down because they were so hungry. We were fighting ISIS, taking care of our injuries, and helping people; all of this together, it was unbelievable, but we managed to do it."

She felt overwhelmed when she saw children who were dying of thirst and hunger. Later, after the corridor had been closed by ISIS attacks and the burning summer had turned to bleak and snowy winter, she witnessed shoeless children living in tents flooded by water and women walking barefoot in dirt and the snow. She wondered how humans could allow this to happen in the twenty-first century. "That's something that will stick in my mind forever," she told me two years later, with a weary expression.

Jidaan Darush led his family onto the Mountain where they drank from muddy pools of water that they found under rocks. Hearing gunshots echoing in the valley, they went up higher. His grandmother was too frail and died in the open. They buried her where she fell.

The plight of the besieged Yezidis came to the world's attention and some relief parcels were dropped by the UK, US, and Iraqi air forces. US Special Forces arrived on the Mountain only to find that many of the Yezidis had already been rescued via the PKK–YPG corridor to Syria.

"When the air drops came everyone ran toward them and some would get something and others wouldn't, which was very difficult," said Sheikh Chele, the custodian of the Yezidi temple of Shebel Qassem, perched on the top of the Mountain. By the temple, there is a graveyard that holds the bodies of dozens of Yezidis who died fighting ISIS during the siege, including children who died of hunger, and those who collapsed from exhaustion and starvation.

"I was sick and terribly sad," remembered Ahmed's mother, Shami Dero, sixty-five, who lost five sons and two grandsons in a single ISIS massacre that morning, on the road north of Tel Azer. She asked anyone who would listen to help her go back to find her sons' bodies but no one would go.

"ISIS fighters have surrounded us; they're everywhere," she was told.

She spent seven days struggling to walk across the Mountain, barely surviving on bottle caps of water given to her by her family. They would move in one direction and then hear it was unsafe and have to take a detour ten kilometers to avoid danger. They slept on rocky ground and begged other Yezidis for bread.

The PKK eventually picked up the family from Kursy, a town on the north side of the Mountain that overlooks tiered fields of tobacco and where Shami was born and married decades before. (Her dowry was an old English rifle that her father later sold to buy a small fig orchard.) They were taken back to Kurdistan.

Ali, the fighter from Siba Sheikheder, hid in the foothills with the help of his Sunni Arab neighbors, who told him he needed to leave after they overheard ISIS in the mosques threatening to convert the Yezidis. Ali drove as far as he could up the Mountain and then abandoned his car, walking with his family for days to Kursy, where they hitched a ride across the ISIS-held desert to Syria.

"You wouldn't want to see your father or brothers there because there was nothing to offer them," he said.

The most dangerous part of the corridor was the open desert near the Syrian border, which was not far from ISIS strongholds. But ISIS was a familiar enemy for the YPG, who had been fighting them for years in Syria.

The first survivors arriving in Iraqi Kurdistan via a river crossing from Syria were distraught, shocked, and exhausted by the heat.

By August 16 most of the trapped civilians had escaped, but the PKK stayed in their Sinjar Mountain bases, even after ISIS blocked their corridor to Syria, and then again after the Peshmerga fought to regain control of the Mountain from the north.

The PKK and YPG's ranks in Sinjar and Rojava swelled with Yezidi recruits who were eager for revenge. Including women and children, whole families took up arms together, with nothing left to lose. Abandoned buildings on the hill slopes became military and ideological training bases adorned with large pictures of Abdullah Öcalan. Although the group espouses gender equality, its fighters worship the image of one man.

Yezidis who made it out to Syria sheltered in the Newroz camp in Rojava, near the town of Derik, seventy miles north of Sinjar. The camp became the first stop for Yezidis fleeing Sinjar. There, many Yezidis, including children, were recruited by the YPG. Thousands more crossed the pontoon bridge back over the Tigris River, sheltering in hastily constructed camps or unfinished buildings left over from the dying economic boom in Iraqi Kurdistan.

As they returned to Iraq, there was at least one town still surrounded by ISIS, its fate as yet undecided.

Part II:
The Women of Kojo

Chapter 5

"He told me about marriage, he told me about love"

The small village of Kojo is fifteen kilometers south of Sinjar, an area famed among Yezidis for its abundant crops and beautiful women. It was here, some fifteen years ago, that "Nadima" waited anxiously for the girl who was passing love notes between herself and Elias, a neighborhood boy. She paid for the messenger girl's secrecy with fruit stolen from her family's farm.

If her parents had known, they wouldn't have approved, even though they were barely in physical contact with each other, apart from quick glances when he visited. Nadima was just fourteen.

"Was it love?" I asked her. She was young and didn't know about such things, she said. "He came to our house and saw me, and then he sent a girl to come and tell me that he liked me." For two years she corresponded secretly with Elias.

Nadima has long black hair tied in a bun, thick eyebrows, and dark, tense eyes. Now in her late twenties, she clearly enjoys talking about her early life, before she had children, when she met and fell in love with her husband, and when one day she tattooed her left hand with a needle and some sheep's milk, before stopping because of the pain.

Nowadays she wears a veil over her hair and dresses entirely in black.

"They were rich and happy," she said of the people from Kojo when she was growing up. "They had good farms with pastures for sheep. Their daughters would grow old and then marry and it would be fine," she said, pointing to the tradition where the bride's family receives a dowry from the family of the groom.

Her parents came from Tel Azer, southeast of Sinjar, and then moved to Kojo because of the town's wells, which provided easy access to water for the farmers on the dry Jazira plain. As a child, Nadima worked on the farm, planting the seeds and digging the ground to grow cucumbers and tomatoes. Their neighbors grew fruit and wheat.

"I was very young and nobody had asked me for a relationship before, he was the first," she said. "He told me about marriage, he told me about love. I told him 'I am very young' and he said 'it's okay—I am also young.'" Elias was older than her by just a year or two.

One day, they arranged to elope. For Yezidis this is a kind of ritual in which couples run away to force marriage negotiations on their families who would otherwise pair their children off in advance. On the set day, Elias sent the messenger girl to Nadima. "He is waiting for you," she said. Together, they traveled to a town north of Kojo where his aunt lived.

Nadima was scared, but she felt confident about her feelings for Elias.

When her family realized she had eloped, they told her she was too young and should come home straightaway: "You have cousins who would like to marry you, and siblings who are older than you and are still unmarried," they said, adding that she could forget about her family if she stayed away. But Nadima didn't budge.

"I'm going to get married so I don't need you," she told them. It took six days for the families to agree to the wedding. Nadima's father asked her fiancé's family for another girl, or one million dinars (around $900) in exchange for her. The groom's family chose the latter and sold some of their sheep to pay the dowry.

While their families negotiated, Nadima stayed with the women of her fiancé's family and Elias stayed with the men. They felt shy when they sat together.

"Everyone else was there so we never really got the chance to be alone," she said. When the agreement was reached, a goat was slaughtered for the wedding feast. Before, Nadima had refused to kiss Elias, but that night, his family told the young couple, "Go and be together."

After the wedding, they stayed with his aunt for two weeks before returning to Kojo, where they had another wedding party. Her family celebrated the marriage by giving her clothes, makeup, and gold jewelry. But as tradition dictates, she then had to say goodbye to them and went to live with her husband's family.

The couple got on well together: they never fought except in jest. Originally a farmer, Elias later got a job working as a guard on the Syrian border. This required him to stay away for ten days at a time, but his new salary meant they no longer had to do farm work.

"When he went away to work, I called him after one day and said 'Now one day is gone, still nine days are left,' and I would tell him 'I miss you.'" On his way home he called to tell her and she celebrated by cooking his favorite food: rice, bulgur wheat, and grilled fish or chicken.

By the time they had their third child, his brothers had also married and the house was too crowded for Nadima. Sometimes she found herself cooking for thirty or forty of his relatives, so in 2011 they moved into their own home. "It was better to be alone," she said. "I married very young, I was as old as her," she said, pointing to her eleven-year-old daughter who sits beside her as we talk. "We had a house, a salary, a car, and life was good—we were very happy."

Much later on, Nadima would see the messenger girl again but under very different circumstances.

--

Leila is also from a family of farmers and shepherds. She is small with a pale, girlish face even though she is twenty-five, and she gives off a kind, practical air. She has two younger sisters and three older brothers. As a child she also worked on the family farm with her brothers, and after a spate of sheep thefts on their ranch, they decided to move closer to Kojo.

Leila said she didn't want to marry so she could stay at home and take care of her mother until her brothers were married. But even when their new wives came and Leila's younger sisters got married, she still chose to stay single. "Not all brains are made the same way," she said. She has suffered from regular fainting fits since she was a child.

In the years after 2003, Leila's brothers joined the Peshmerga, and she remembers that on August 2, 2014, their colleagues in Siba Sheikheder called and asked for help. By mid-morning on August 3, the Peshmerga stationed in Kojo had fled. In the confusion, Leila's family and around one hundred others decided to run away from the town, but most people stayed, unsure what was going to happen to them.

Leila's younger sister was living in Siba Sheikheder with her new husband and phoned home to her parents on that morning: "We're running—ISIS is coming," she said. They drove north to Sinjar, leaving her uncle at home to guard the house. Arriving in Sinjar, they realized the city was already under attack and its people were running. Gathering together in a patch of scrubland outside Sinjar, they phoned her uncle.

"Is it safe to return?" they asked him.

"They've surrounded us and won't let us leave," he said. Neither option would be safe. They were now trapped. Shortly after the phone call, a group of ISIS fighters approached them and told them to hand over money, guns, gold, and phones. Leila remembers that the leader had a red face and beard and was called "emir" ("prince") by the others.

Fighters drove her family to one of the central government offices in Sinjar, where the ID cards used to be issued. What seemed like thousands of women and girls had been gathered inside the building's offices, men crammed together on the second floor. At around 9 p.m. that evening ISIS guards brought lanterns inside and began inspecting the faces of the women and girls. The women huddled together for protection, and as the men drew near to Leila, she was so scared that she fainted. This saved her from being taken away that night. Five of her female cousins were not so lucky.

The Yezidi women in Sinjar didn't realize it yet, but the ISIS fighters were carrying out a preplanned mass abduction for the purpose of institutionalized rape. Initially they were looking for unmarried women and girls over eight.

--

In the months following the capture of Sinjar, ISIS released an article in their online magazine *Dabiq* that attempted to justify taking the female "spoils of war" as a return to early Islam.[61]

Under the title "The Revival of Slavery Before the Hour," the author describes the Yezidis as pagans and devil worshippers who are not entitled to pay a tax and live in the caliphate. In this they are unlike Christians, who are considered "people of the book." The piece goes on to say that the Yezidis' "continual existence to this day is a matter that Muslims should question as they will be asked about it on Judgment Day."[62]

The article describes how, before taking Sinjar, ISIS students of Islamic law were asked to research the Yezidis to determine the way they should be treated. The author then looks to the Koran and Hadith for mentions of slavery practiced in the early days of Islam, referencing a prophecy attributed to the Prophet, which says that one sign of the coming of the day of judgment will be when the slave gives birth to her master.

"ISIS's culture of enslavement, encompassing acts and rhetoric, functions precisely by (selective) appeal to the Muslim tradition, as well as deliberate inversion of widespread moral norms," wrote Dr. Kecia Ali in her book *Sexual Ethics and Islam: Feminist Reflections on Qur'an, Hadith, and Jurisprudence.*[63]

ISIS sees the reintroduction of slavery as part of a return to a supposedly purer, earlier version of the faith, via their partial reading of Islamic law. An ISIS pamphlet on slavery states:

"It is not allowed to lie carnally with them or enjoy them simply for being sabi [captive], but also the Imam must make divisions among them [and thus] if they are allowed to be taken as slave girls, the possessions of one's right hand, then one can lie carnally with them according to Shari'i [Islamic law] conditions."[64]

A whole theory of property around the Yezidi captives emerged.

Another document released online in late 2014 in the form of a question and answer session provides rules for keeping slaves, and states that it is permissible to have a sex with a slave before puberty "if she is fit for intercourse; however, if she is not fit for intercourse, then it is enough to enjoy her without intercourse." The document details what captives should wear to pray and how a man should act toward another man's slave.[65]

Rape is a common weapon of war and has been used across the globe to destroy enemies physically and psychologically. ISIS' own documents acknowledge that this was their aim. The pamphlet said:

"For God has struck the disbelievers who have violated the command of God...and among the sins of this humiliation imposed on them is the captivity and enslavement of their women and the permissibility of their genitals. And this is an objective in angering and psychologically vanquishing the disbelievers when they see their honor as captives among the people of Islam, and it is of disgrace for them."

The author of the *Dabiq* article writes that if the slave becomes a believer she should be freed. But the idea of showing mercy to the enslaved women was not carried out in practice.

--

In jails across Iraq and Syria, where the women were now being held, they felt a sense of "abject terror on hearing footsteps in the corridor outside and keys opening the locks," said a report by the UN Commission for the Inquiry on Syria that designated the ISIS crimes against the Yezidis' genocide. "The first twelve hours of capture were filled with sharply mounting terror. Many of the women and children had seen or heard their male relatives being killed by the armed ISIS fighters who now surrounded them.

"The selection of any girl was accompanied by screaming as she was forcibly pulled from the room, with her mother and any other women who tried to keep hold of her being brutally beaten by fighters. [Yezidi] women and girls began to scratch and bloody themselves in an attempt to make themselves unattractive to potential buyers."

At first, the women and girls were taken to prearranged locations in Iraq where they were handed out to the ISIS fighters who took part in the attack on Sinjar.[66] To avoid being raped, some of the girls killed themselves by slitting their wrists or throats, or hanging themselves, or throwing themselves from buildings in Tel Afar, Mosul, and Raqqa.

Amid the panic in the Sinjar ID office, Leila decided to pose as a mother to her small niece and nephew after she saw the other women being taken away, and correctly assumed that being unmarried was dangerous.

The following day, the Yezidi men on the second floor disappeared.

Leila was transported east to a school-turned-prison in Tel Afar where the women were crowded into classrooms that now functioned as cells, guarded by fighters who continued to pick out beautiful girls to serve as slaves. Each time they were moved, their names and ages were noted down on a list.

Chapter 6

"We asked him to destroy her"

"Zahra" from Kojo has quick, darting eyes and a low voice. When she was young, her father, a former Iraqi soldier, died in a car crash. Her two brothers went to primary school, but the family was too poor to educate all three daughters, so just one of Zahra's sisters joined them.

"She was smart and she knew many things," Zahra said a little wistfully of her sister, who is still missing. Instead of going to school, Zahra worked on local farms to bring back money for her family. She isn't sure of her exact age, guessing she is between seventeen and twenty-seven. After finishing school, her brothers went to work as day laborers in the Kurdistan region.

On August 3, 2014, her brothers were all back at home visiting.

Some villagers, like Leila, fled, but most stayed and, by late afternoon, Kojo was surrounded and no one else could leave. ISIS fighters, identified by survivors as Sunnis from the local Khawatina tribe and surrounding villages, took away the weapons belonging to Yezidi men. Abu Hamza, an Iraqi Arab from the Jazira desert, came to the town to negotiate with local leaders on behalf of ISIS.

Abu Hamza's convoys visited Kojo regularly during the next ten days as the men in the village tried to negotiate a safe passage to the Mountain. In one meeting, ISIS told them they would have to convert or be killed. Unlike in other towns, they were given time to think over their decision.

Nadima, the former runaway teenage bride, stayed in Kojo with her husband and four children, pregnant with her fifth. One night, Yezidis from a nearby town fled to the Mountain. ISIS surrounded Kojo to make sure its inhabitants didn't do the same thing.

On August 15, ISIS told the villagers to gather in the local school at midday. The women were told to go to the second floor. "They took everything from us: gold, cell phones, car keys, and afterwards they took all the men outside," said Zahra. When the women came downstairs they saw blankets laid out on the floor—one with cell phones and one with wallets.

The village elder, or mukhtar, of Kojo, Ahmed Jasso, was in one of the last groups to be taken outside and executed. One woman told an investigator that she saw the mukhtar when she came down the stairs. "There's nothing more I can do," he said, as he was taken away.

The men had chosen to remain Yezidi and were paying for it with their lives.

They were driven in groups of ten to fifteen to just outside the town where they were lined up in ditches and shot. When they exited the cars and knew they were going to die, they gathered in a huddle and recited the last testament—affirmation that they were the people of Melek Tawuse, the peacock angel, God's representative on earth.

A handful of men survived the executions by pretending to be dead, lying under the bodies of their neighbors. ISIS fighters stood over them and came back, once and then twice, to shoot anyone who was still moving. One survivor, hiding under the dead, remembers recognizing the gunmen from the Mutaywit tribe, whose tribal area surrounds Kojo.

"For a long time we've lived together so when these people came, we could understand their accents," the survivor said. Another man from Kojo who had already escaped to Kurdistan was receiving phone calls about the executions from a Sunni neighbor. He reported that a few survivors had arrived at his farm, and that ISIS had piled earth on the corpses of the others using bulldozers.

Zahra hasn't heard from her two brothers since these events. They were loved by everyone, she said. "I wish I knew what happened to them."

Over five hundred men and boys were executed on that day. The killings in Kojo were the worst massacre committed against the Yezidis that August. Men who survived remember seeing an aircraft flying above them as they played dead in the ditches, waiting for nightfall and for their executioners to leave.

What they saw was probably a US military drone that conducted two air strikes on ISIS vehicles near Kojo that evening after receiving reports about what was happening from Kurdish forces. But by then the massacres had already taken place.[67]

"After they finished with the men, they used our own cars and started moving us from Kojo to the technical institute in Solagh," said Zahra, referring to a building in the east of Sinjar. "All that's left of Kojo are the people you see here in this camp," she said, pointing to a collection of squat trailers parked below the hills. She estimates about six hundred people are lost, killed, or kidnapped from her town. "We are in touch with about fifty [of those kidnapped] at the most."

In the technical institute, the women and girls were divided up by age, and the younger women and girls, including Zahra and her two sisters, were driven by bus to a wedding hall in Mosul. Known as the Galaxy Hall, it had been a smart venue in its prime, situated in a wooded area on the eastern side of the Tigris River.

On August 16, more than eighty older women from Kojo were massacred behind the technical institute. Their bodies were thrown in a dried-up fish pond. Years later, their clothes and bones were still visible. The son of one woman murdered there showed me her picture later. Noora Ismail, sixty-five, sits in the middle of a yellow and green meadow, a blue sky above. She wears a long white skirt with an orange sash and looks calm and relaxed. The picture was taken on a family picnic. When I visited the mass grave over a year later I saw a similar orange sash lying in the dirt.[68]

--

The Galaxy Hall was guarded by Iraqi ISIS fighters wearing gray or camouflaged tunics. Inside there were kitchens, dressing rooms, and toilets that previously would have been used for party guests to reapply makeup or comb their hair. Now the Yezidi women like Zahra cowered in these rooms, fearful and anxious. Some managed to keep their mobile phones and had heard from others outside that women were being sold as slaves.

Historically Yezidi women who converted or married beyond the faith were banished, and many of the girls in the hall wanted to kill themselves rather than be cast out by their families if they tried to return.

Manjie and her family were moved to the Galaxy Hall a few months after she was captured on the road leading up to the Mountain. When she arrived, ISIS women came to inspect them, peeking under their headscarves and taking any gold jewelry.

They were looking for unmarried girls, and threatened virginity tests if they thought the women were lying to them.

Manjie's sixteen-year-old stepdaughter was pretending to be married to one of their male relatives, but Manjie was scared that the lie would be discovered and she would be taken away.

One night, as the other hostages lay sleeping, Manjie and her husband's first wife woke up the sleeping girl and made her go into a bathroom cubicle with the man pretending to be her husband. The women told them to have sex so ISIS wouldn't take her away.

"I begged them to do it. We asked him to destroy her," she said. "It was strange, but they are Yezidi so it is all right."

"You've become my pimp!" her daughter cried.

"What could I do?" Manjie told me later. "I didn't have another solution."

The wives forced the young couple into the bathroom cubicle, and her mother gave her a sanitary napkin to collect the drops of blood—traditionally a white sheet is used—to prove she was a virgin before.

"We destroyed her," Manjie said sadly. "She was crying all the time. She was in pain and hurt."

The women said they had to force the couple to have sex to avoid a greater evil: the loss of the girl's virginity to a non-Yezidi (historically this would result in the Yezidi woman being cast out of the community). Afterward the man was too embarrassed to stay with the family and went to sit with the other men.

Another man in the hall was screaming and crying about his two daughters, and asking any young man to please take them. "I don't want a dowry. I don't want anything. Just take them—they are yours. At least it is our honor. You are Yezidis and my daughters should be taken by a Yezidi man," he called out as he wept.

Manjie's husband's first wife still has the white napkin her daughter used to collect the blood. "It was a sanitary towel because we didn't have another piece of white cloth," she explained. "I took it with me to Tel Afar, Deir ez-Zor, and Raqqa [in Syria] and I kept it with me here," she said, pointing to her chest with a small, sad smile.

Zahra spent only one night in the Galaxy Hall. The next day four large buses arrived to take her and the other Yezidi girls from Kojo to Syria. It was not yet light when they were forced onto the bus. They cried throughout the ten-hour trip to Raqqa.

The speed with which Zahra was taken to Syria suggests that markets and jails for the women had already been established. Compared to married women with children, single women were moved at greater speed through ISIS markets that favored more saleable slaves.

--

Raqqa, 370 kilometers west of Mosul in northern Syria, became ISIS' de facto capital, and supporters from all over the world flocked there to join the group via the Turkish border. It was also the destination for Zahra and the other women from Sinjar.

"When we got to the farm [near Raqqa] we saw four or five buses full of ISIS members with long hair and beards," said Zahra. "They were like animals. On the first day they came among us and started picking girls for themselves. Two or three of them would catch the girls, blindfold them, and take them by force into a car. The girls were crying and shouting and wailing but they didn't care."

From the second floor of the building, the girls could see the Euphrates River, but they were hidden from view by the surrounding trees and fences.

"We were just like sheep, when the shepherd goes toward them and the sheep disperse; that's how we were, running away from them." Zahra fled when the men came but she was blocked by a fence at the edge of the farm. On the first day the men took between twenty and forty girls. Food was delivered from a local restaurant for those who remained, but they were too scared to eat.

They covered their faces with ash to try and look unattractive in the hope they wouldn't be picked.

After two days, Zahra and her sister were taken to an underground ISIS prison in Raqqa. Hundreds of women were crammed into three rooms in what was just one of several similar structures that were used for holding women in Raqqa.

The girls arrived at night and weren't allowed to see the outside of the building—a tactic similar to that used on prisoners by the Syrian government in its jails, said Sareta Ashraph, former chief analyst with the UN Commission of Inquiry on Syria.

Inside the prison the women had to share a few filthy, overflowing toilets, forcing them to stand in raw sewage. Their bodies were crawling with sand flies. The only light came from two solar-powered lamps hanging from the ceiling, one prisoner recalled. Each morning the guards would give them a small piece of bread and cheese to share between two, and in the evening some rice and soup.

Some women sat on bags or clothes to try to avoid touching the filthy ground. Children cried constantly with hunger. The women waited under the constant fear or rape or death. "They were always beating us and we had diarrhea because of the fear," said "Khulka," who had arrived at the prison with her four children, inside a refrigerator truck normally used for ice cream. She is thirty years old and comes from the town of Tel Qasab.

"We didn't have a shower for one month and we always had lice in our hair. . . . After two months they took us outside but we couldn't stand because we hadn't seen the sun for so long."

While in the jail, Khulka tattooed herself with the names of her husband and father so that her body could be recognized and returned to them if she was killed.

"We did it with needles. The blood would go here on our hands, but we said, let us die."

She mixed the breast milk from a lactating woman with ash, and used a needle she smuggled inside the jail. With the same needle and some thread, she began embroidering her underwear with the names and numbers listed in her phone in case ISIS found it and took it away. Khulka had been to school, and unlike many of the women there, she knew how to read and write. She began sewing other women's clothes with their loved ones' names and numbers so that they would not be forgotten.

In 2007, 72 percent of women in Sinjar district had received less than a primary education, much higher than the rate for men, and 57 percent of women were illiterate. In the years before 2014, literacy rates were improving in Sinjar, but many women and girls worked in the fields to support their families while their brothers went to school. Illiteracy made it harder for women to escape after they were taken into captivity because they couldn't read the signs on unfamiliar buildings in ISIS-held towns and cities.

Historically, Yezidis eschewed formal education that was associated with repressive state authorities, languages, and the threat of conversion. The tradition faded, but its impact can still be seen in the female illiteracy rate.

Khulka was taken to a side room in the prison with her children and photographed by the ISIS guards who gave her the slave number 16, which was then printed above her photo. There were around five hundred women in the jail, she recalls, and all of them had to pose with their children and were given slave numbers. Before the picture was taken, she cut her daughter's hair to make her look like a boy and stop them being separated. If the guards recognized her daughter as a young girl there was more chance she'd be taken. The other imprisoned women were jealous of Khulka's gray hair, thinking it might save her from being seized. They tried to imitate it using ash.

"Some of these women and girls resisted forced conversion, protected themselves against violence or at least tried to, and protected their children. How they resisted really shows incredible intelligence, courage, and strength," said human rights lawyer and gender justice advocate Sherizaan Minwalla.

Yezidi women, who fled what is now Turkey in the final years of the Ottoman Empire during the First World War and the chaos that followed, passed down stories that are repeated among Sinjaris today. Among them are accounts of how they did what Khulka was now doing: covering their daughters' faces with ash and cutting their hair to try to stop them being enslaved.

In the same prison, Zahra and her sisters were put together into small rooms. They heard screaming and crying as ISIS guards came in the middle of the night to drag away the girls. The guards came for Zahra's middle sister first. When Zahra pleaded with them not to take them separately, one of the guards whipped her with a cable.

Such violence inflicted in prisons was, of course, commonplace at the hands of ISIS. After they were rescued with the help of Kurdish and US Special Forces, prisoners from an ISIS jail in Iraq told me about other violent abuse.[69] Abu Wahid, one of the prisoners held in an ISIS jail in Hawija, was accused of passing secrets to the Kurds in northern Iraq: "First, they brought me to a room, sat me down, and put water on me. Next, they brought electricity cables and applied a charge to my neck. For the next three days, blood would come from my mouth when I slept.

"When I felt dizzy and passed out because I couldn't take any more, they brought the cables to wake me up again." During his captivity, Abu Wahid heard other prisoners being taken outside and shot, and was told he would be next, before the raid that saved him.

After her sister was taken from the cell, the door opened again and this time Zahra was grabbed by two large men and shoved into a car. "I won't go until you give me my sister!" she cried out. The men didn't listen and instead drove her to a house in Raqqa belonging to a man called Abu Tabuq.

Chapter 7

"I would burn him alive"

Nadima, the former teenage runaway bride, spent four months in Tel Afar after the August attack. Here, her eldest daughter, who was eleven, was taken away to live with a middle-aged ISIS man and his wife and children. He brought her back a few times on visits, but they had only a few minutes together. On one visit, she told her mother that she was too afraid to cry out loud in their house. Instead, she would put a blanket over her head and bite her finger so she wouldn't make a sound while she wept. Soon after, her daughter was taken to Syria and Nadima didn't hear from her again.

When winter came, Nadima was moved to an underground jail in Raqqa, and then to a nearby military base run by a local "wali," or governor, who was in charge of buying and selling the women. She was heavily pregnant with her fifth child, but this didn't stop the wali from beating her when she tried to fight him off before he raped her.

As the birth of her child approached, the wali sent her with a driver to Manbij, a city in northeastern Syria not far from the Turkish border. Her driver was given a note to take to the emir (prince) of Manbij that noted her age, condition, and the fact that she was a Yezidi slave.

The driver took her to the main hospital in Manbij, where the emir read the note and sent her to have an ultrasound scan with a female nurse. She was due to give birth in two weeks. The emir installed her in an apartment on the fifth floor of a building close to the hospital, along with her three children, to await the birth.

Part of the emir's job was to stamp and sign official documents that allowed citizens of the Islamic State to travel. He also oversaw marriage contracts and organized the purchasing of medicine for the hospital. Later, during the fight to retake Manbij, the US announced the capture of a US headquarters in the city, located in a hospital used as an ISIS logistics hub and command center.[70]

Two weeks later, in January 2015, Nadima gave birth in the Manbij hospital. Afterward, the emir called the wali who had sent her and asked if he should send her back to him. "She is a gift. You're free to do what you like with her," the wali replied.

The emir decided to keep her for himself. Nadima was now his property. She was also a single mother looking after four children, including a newborn baby. She didn't know what had happened to her husband, Elias, the man who had first sent her love notes. He disappeared when they were separated at the school in Kojo.

The emir lived with his family in the city and came to the apartment to rape Nadima every week. When he left, he locked the door behind him so she couldn't escape. Every few days, some food would be dropped off for her and the children, but it was never enough.

--

From Tel Afar, Leila was moved to Badoush prison, northwest of Mosul, for a month, and then she was moved to a village south of Tel Afar called Qasr Mihrab. Here, ISIS gathered large numbers of Yezidi hostages and put them in homes previously abandoned by the town's Shia residents who had fled or were killed when ISIS took over. Leila was still pretending that her five-year-old niece was her daughter.

Four checkpoints surrounded the village and each one was guarded by three local Sunni Turkmen who brought stale food for the Yezidi. The Yezidis in the village had supposedly converted to Islam and were put to work loading hay and taking care of cows and sheep. One woman's job was making yogurt for the

ISIS fighters. The men had to attend the mosque five times a day to pray. The women were supposed to pray at home.

Despite these "conversions," ISIS fighters would beat the hostages and continued to come among them and choose young women and girls to take away. When the guards entered the area where the Yezidis lived, the girls would run away to hide. Leila and her cousins hid among the trees, behind the house, or in the cow shed, until the men departed.

Some Yezidis managed to escape to Sinjar, thirty kilometers east, by walking through the night across muddy fields, keeping to the valleys to avoid ISIS checkpoints and reach the Peshmerga.

This was the time that the Yezidis could most feasibly have been rescued by negotiation or diplomacy. The captives were held together and some still had mobile phones hidden under their clothes to call relatives back in Kurdistan and tell them exactly where they were. But with little in the way of rapid international or governmental support materializing, a sense of abandonment soon grew among the families waiting for their loved ones.

Instead, a black market run by Yezidi smugglers became active in rescuing women and guiding the slaves by phone through the night and then collecting them at the front lines. The smugglers were mostly businessmen who had been trading in farming equipment and other goods. One was a lawyer. They were men with connections, who, after the ISIS attacks, began using their networks of friends and contacts in Arab Iraq and Syria to negotiate and arrange for the recapture or purchasing of slaves from ISIS. For the few months after ISIS attacked Sinjar, this was easier. But as time went on, and women were dispersed, the rescue missions became much harder.

"Within days of what happened to the Yezidis on the Mountain the phone calls went from 'help us survive' to 'they've kidnapped these women and can you help us to rescue them,'" said Thomas Malinowski, former US Assistant Secretary, Bureau of Democracy, Human Rights, and Labor, interviewed while he was still in post during a visit to Erbil, the capital of the Kurdistan region.

"Hostage rescues are one of the most dangerous things to do, but when they [the women] were still being held in large groups this was discussed, but tragically they were then dispersed. . . . It is still very much on our minds and something we know has to be considered."

To date there have been no known, large-scale rescue missions to free the Yezidi captives in Iraq and Syria, by either the US, Iraqi, or Kurdistan regional governments.

Perhaps because of the high number of escapes from the town, or because their "conversions" were not seen as genuine, the hostages kept in villages around Tel Afar were separated. Women, like Leila, were taken to Syria to be sold, and the men disappeared, probably having been killed: "The Peshmerga were advancing now and the captives were a military threat to ISIS," as a group within the caliphate who were in touch with the enemy by phone, said the UN's Sareta Ashraph.

Leila was now on her way along the highway to Syria. She arrived at the farm in Raqqa more than six months after Zahra had left. Hundreds of women and girls were there when Leila arrived, some, like her, posing as mothers to children that were not their own to hide the fact they were single.

The house at the farm was large but so crowded that the women had to sleep in shifts. "If I was tired or sick I would sleep for fifteen minutes to an hour and then I would wake up and another one would take my place." The only furniture was cardboard boxes; the blankets were so dirty that Leila couldn't look at them. They were fed one portion of rice or one potato with a piece of bread daily.

One night she was assaulted by an old Syrian guard who regularly came amongst the girls, picking one to take off to a side room and abuse. She was on her period, "so he didn't manage to take my honor," she said, but her screams were heard by the other captives, and later, when she removed her shirt, her chest could be seen as heavily bruised.

When an ISIS leader visited a week later, the girls tried to complain about the abuse from the guards, but the leader shrugged off their complaints. Aside from isolated incidents, mass rape was uncommon at the holding sites in Mosul and Tel Afar before the women were sold to ISIS members. This shows the hold ISIS had on its fighters. The enslavement wasn't purely about unconstrained sexual need; there were rules in place to guarantee the organization and purchase of the slave women in the market system.[71]

For most of the women and girls over the age of nine, sexual assault began when they were sold to an ISIS fighter. Along with being sexually abused, they were expected to work as domestic slaves. They were regularly beaten and forbidden to go outside. Most were not allowed to cook because, as "disbelievers," their food was viewed by ISIS as being unclean. Escape attempts were often punished by gang rape.

--

According to ISIS, it has no choice but to attack and kill disbelieving men. Flowing from this, it justifies the enslaving of their women as an act of protection, a way of replacing the men who previously looked after them. This idea is crucial to the role of slavery in ISIS' conception of how a caliphate should function.

Implicit in this is the goal of eliminating the Yezidi community, the idea that that society would be better without them, which is common to all genocides, said former UN investigator Sareta Ashraph. The enslavement, for ISIS, is meant to eventually bring the women to Islam, and is part of their ideology of conquest. "[It is] among the greatest forms of the honor of Islam and its Sharia [Islamic law], as it is a clear affirmation showing the supremacy of the people of Sharia, and the greatness of their affairs, and the dominance of their state, and the power of their might," according to the ISIS pamphlet on slavery.[72]

ISIS describes its own use of enslavement through a mix of clumsy metaphors about sex, war, and power. Dividing up the captive women and children among the ISIS mujahideen (holy warriors) and "sanctioning their genitals" is described as a sign of "realization and dominance by the sword."[73]

Dr. Katherine E. Brown, lecturer in Islamic Studies at Birmingham University, explained that ISIS mainly justifies its use of slavery through selective interpretations of the Hadith, the reported accounts of the life and sayings of the Prophet Muhammad and his companions:

"They justify it on the basis that it is a reward for carrying out services for the community—slaves are presented as compensation for fighters. However, they chose particular ways of seeing these Hadith and selectively choose them so as to ignore, for example, the requirement not to kill your prisoners by focusing on the requirement to make sure they 'don't escape' by being 'secured at the neck' until negotiations have taken place."

Keeping slaves was common throughout the ancient world, as well as in (but not limited to) Islamic societies up until the nineteenth and twentieth centuries, when the practice was abolished. Slavery was acknowledged in the Koran as a fact of life at the time, when the practice was mainly a preserve of the elites who could afford to keep concubines.[74] The practice has clearly fallen out of favor among modern Muslims as it has among those from other religions whose holy books endorsed slavery, such as Christians and Jews. Nevertheless, though illegal, modern-day slavery continues across the globe.

The promise of sexual slavery is used as a sweetener when recruiting disaffected young men to ISIS, while, at the same time, stories about sex and violence in the media involving non-Muslim women being enslaved by Muslim men feed stereotypes about Muslim men that then create divisions that ISIS can then exploit.[75]

"Slavery serves to increase the ISIS community because Yezidi women will give birth and the children will be brought up among its fighters," writes the author of the ISIS pamphlet on slavery.[76]

By enslaving thousands of Yezidi women, ISIS may have dealt a lasting demographic blow to the community, already limited by the prohibition on marriage outside the faith and between their own castes. The group's ambition was also to use Yezidi women as incubators for "true" ISIS members, thereby replacing Yezidis with their own people and culture.

The same document calls on fighters to be good to their slaves, citing words from the Koran calling for them to be good to "those whom your right hand possess"—a euphemism for a female captive—and cites Islamic texts with instructions not to hit the slave's face, and to emancipate the slave who becomes a believer, for which the master will be rewarded by God.

But, as with other strictures, there is a gap between ISIS proclamations and an abusive, often violent reality.[77] Many rules, such as waiting to make sure an enslaved women isn't pregnant before sleeping with her, or giving her enough to eat, were regularly broken.

ISIS fighters used contraception, including the forced administration if birth control medication, to guarantee a woman could continue being available for sex, showing the importance of economic realities in the slave markets, over ideologies of expanding the Muslim population (this was also apparent later when fighters began ransoming women back to their families for large amounts of money). Although most of the women and girls weren't sure exactly how much they were sold for, anecdotally the more children a woman had, the less desirable she would be and the longer she would wait in ISIS prisons.

ISIS used gang rape as punishment for women and girls who tried to escape to further degrade and control them physically and psychologically. Despite this, many of the women continued to fight back against their captors, risking punishment and death in pursuit of freedom.

After the women were captured, they didn't immediately become slaves to the fighters, but were held for a period whilst their details were recorded. The process was systematized. Women were then sold in markets, either electronically over a mobile phone messenger app where their photos and slave numbers were exchanged, or in market halls and prisons at prearranged times. Away from the main markets, women and girls, supplied by fighters or ISIS members who acted as middlemen, were sold by local brokers in smaller numbers. At the beginning, they were given mainly to Iraqi fighters who took part in the battle for Sinjar. Subsequently, the remaining captives were taken to Syria, and sold there, often to fighters who had arrived from around the world.

A document from Homs governorate in western Syria in mid-2015 gives instruction for ISIS fighters who want Yezidi women.[78] The "Statement for Distribution" was sent to battalions and sectors under "the military administration," and the offices associated with "the matters of the mujahideen (marriage office)."

It tells fighters to register their names with the "admin official of the battalion sector," and says that for those currently fighting on the front line, arrangements will be made with the emir of their battalion: "And whoever does not register his name has no right to attend the 'slave trade market.' And the bid is to be submitted in the sealed envelope at the time of purchase, and the one who wins the bid is obliged to purchase."

In late 2014, a group of young, bearded men sat on long sofas lining the walls of a living room somewhere in the caliphate, wearing ammunition-packed vests. They joked with one another. "Tomorrow is the slave market, God willing," said one of the men, as he flashed a grin at his companions. "You can sell your slave, or give her as a gift. . . . You can do whatever you want with your share," said another fighter in view of the cameraman who was recording the exchange. The men didn't seem to notice and continued discussing buying women for "three banknotes or a pistol."

"It costs more for one with blue eyes."

"Check her teeth."

"Can one take two slave girls? Does that work?" the fighter asks his friends.

"Abu Fahd, your [Yezidi] is dead!" someone giggles.[79]

--

"It was a big room full of chairs, like a hall," recalled a thirty-one-year-old Yezidi woman describing an underground market in the central Syrian town of Palmyra. She was taken to the slave market with her eight-year-old daughter, along with twenty-one other Yezidi slave women. "There were many ISIS members there, sitting on the chairs," she recalled.

"Next to the large room was a smaller room where all the women and children were; they would come and take one group at a time, a woman with her children, to the bigger room. When they moved us from the smaller room to the bigger room they would make us perform like we were in a fashion show and make us walk from this side to that side and all the ISIS men were looking at us. They ran a lottery on the computer to pick the most beautiful ones. They did this by inputting the names of seven or eight ISIS members who wanted that lady, and then a winner would be chosen automatically. The women were screaming and crying, and my daughter was so scared that she went very white."

There were up to 250 men in the room when it was her turn to appear. After she was sold, along with her daughter, she was locked away for three months and made to work as a domestic slave, before being moved to Aleppo province. In Palmyra she became suicidal.

"What kept me going during that time was my daughter," she said. "At one point, I wanted to kill her and myself. She stopped sleeping because she was so worried I was going to do it. That was the worst moment."

--

After just a little more than a month at the farm, Leila and three other girls from Kojo were taken back to Iraq and kept in a military base near the Iraq–Syria border, more than two hundred kilometers south of Sinjar in Anbar province. Two girls were sold to an Anbari sheikh and the third to an unknown man. After they left, two more Yezidi girls from Sinjar were brought to the base to replace them.

The military base was in Al-Qa'im, a border crossing between Iraq and Syria, although under the caliphate it was now merely a pit stop between ISIS-held stretches of desert. It was also a common crossing point for slaves passing between markets in ISIS towns and cities.

Leila was sold to Muhammed, who looked familiar to her. Then she remembered who he was: his family were from the large Shammar tribal confederation and were kriefs, like godparents to her family.

Leila's family farm was next door to Muhammed's when they were growing up. Her mom and aunt used to bake bread for his family and her uncle would invite the men to eat with them in their home. "Our lands were very close to each other, there was only one road between them," she told me. Sometimes Leila's dad would take care of Muhammed's sheep.

When Leila saw Muhammed, she felt relieved and thought that perhaps he would rescue her and sell her back to her family. "I recognized him but he didn't recognize me. I told him I am [name redacted]'s daughter." Muhammed didn't say anything. He just looked shocked and left the room. When he came back his face was covered with a scarf and only his eyes were showing. "But I still knew him," she said. The next day Muhammed came back and told Leila he had sold her on again.

"It's fine to sell me," she said, "everyone does."

In one of Leila's old family photos, Muhammed's brother sits on the floor with a group of men wearing long white robes and eating from a huge pile of meat and rice in the center of the room. "He is our krief," Leila's cousin said, inside their small tent, pointing to Muhammed's brother in the picture. "Muhammed sold Leila to an ISIS member for $1,500. If I see him again I will drink his blood," he said, drawing his thumb slowly across his throat and lifting his thumb up to his mouth as if he was drinking.

Three days later, Leila was taken to a military base near Ramadi and sold to a notorious Anbari ISIS military commander. It was early 2015 and she would stay in the base for one month. Later, when she had escaped and was in Baghdad, someone asked her what she would do if she saw Muhammed again. "I would burn him alive," she said.

Chapter 8

"All those ISIS motherfuckers are no good"

Zahra was locked in Abu Tabuq's house in Raqqa. The house next door was full of weapons and ammunition and was one of five large armories across the city. Abu Tabuq was a twenty-nine-year-old man with long hair and a thin, light-colored beard. He made her clean the house and wash his clothes, while he worked at an Islamic State center that distributed weapons to fighters.

At first he was cruel and raped her, but when she began to obey his orders, he was a little kinder toward her. He explained that her conversion to Islam was dependent on an ISIS member "marrying" (raping) her, after which she would become a true Muslim. "Fuck their mother's religion!" she said angrily when recounting this, her eyes flaring. "Even when I was praying in the Islamic way I would pray to my own religion inside. When I was in front of them I would say what they liked, but if they weren't there I would do it my way."

She survived by retaining the belief that she would go back to her own religion eventually. "I never took their advice—it went in one ear and out the other." Abu Tabuq told her to forget about her past, her family, and her religion: "The only thing you have to care about is me," he said.

If she didn't obey him he would beat her. As a member of ISIS, he had been morally corrupted and wasn't capable of being truly kind, she explained. "Sometimes he brought me clothes that were full of blood to wash." She washed the bloodstained clothes three, four times, trying to remove the stains from what were probably the clothes of dead fighters.

"All those ISIS motherfuckers are no good. Because of those bastards many young Yezidi girls have killed themselves.

"They could do anything they liked with us, we were just like sheep. Compare my case to others and I didn't go through a lot. Yes, I was bought and sold but in other cases they were bought and sold maybe fifteen times."

She had been in Raqqa for around four months, mostly spent in Abu Tabuq's house, when he sold her to Abu Mawa, a thirty-eight-year-old Libyan ISIS fighter living in Deir ez-Zor in eastern Syria. Abu Mawa drove her from Raqqa in a yellow taxi.

When they arrived, he gave her revealing clothes to put on for him. She refused, and as punishment, he broke her leg with a metal bar.

The next day, for her impertinence, Abu Mawa sold her to another Libyan fighter known as Abu Adafa. He was only eighteen years old. He was living in the same compound full of caravans near the Conoco gas processing plant, south of Deir ez-Zor, where many Libyan ISIS fighters were based at the time. He was so young that he couldn't grow a moustache, and rather than raping and beating her like the other fighters, he decided that it was his mission to convert her to Islam and teach her about the message of the Koran.

Many Yezidi girls were by now being held in the same compound of one hundred to two hundred caravans where the Libyan fighters lived. Their descriptions of the place are all eerily similar. The women and girls were chained, beaten, raped, and passed around like animals between the men. At the edge of the compound, a barbed-wire fence prevented them from escaping. In the day, the men went to fight, but Abu Mawa stayed at the entrance to keep guard.

When Zahra arrived, the other women asked her why she was there. "I had no choice," she told them. The women and girls there were covered in bruises, had broken hands and swollen eyes. They tended to be younger captives, from Kojo and some from Sinjar city.

Zahra tried hard to memorize passages from the Koran and points of Islamic law for Abu Adafa, and when she applied herself, he was gentler with her. "When I tried hard he was happy," she said, and thankfully, unlike the other men, he didn't hit her.

Slowly, they got to know each other. Zahra told him the story of her kidnap, and explained how she had ended up in Deir ez-Zor. Abu Adafa was surprised that she had been forcibly enslaved and thought they had chosen to convert. "He thought that we had come with our own free will. Because of this, he regretted joining ISIS; he didn't realize before that the group was that bad."

The young man was extremely religious and decided not to rape Zahra because he believed it would lessen his sins in the eyes of God at judgment day and increase his chances of entering Paradise. As they got to know each other, Zahra questioned him about why ISIS was kidnapping and enslaving women, and why the fighters were buying and selling them. He told her that they had no choice and had been ordered to do so.

He continued to show some empathy for her: he became sad and regretful when he heard how she had been treated by other men, although he refused to say anything to the other fighters. The men of ISIS had a code of "honor" that meant they couldn't interfere in another man's relationship with slaves—even if the man murdered his slave girl, no one could say anything to him.

--

The Yezidi women and girls in Deir ez-Zor were scared about the stigma of rape in their own community. The conversions to Islam were forced on them, but with no way to communicate with the outside world, they didn't know if they would ever be accepted back, if they did manage to escape from the hellish cycle of buying, selling, torture, and rape.

"We were so worried. We thought: how will we face our families? Some even said 'if we go back they might reject or kill us.' Some girls killed themselves because they didn't want to face their families."

When the first Yezidi women began escaping and returned to Iraqi Kurdistan, the religious authority, Baba Sheikh, ignored the dictates of tradition. The women would be accepted back despite having been forced to convert, or raped by ISIS fighters. "I decide to accept them myself, along with the [Yezidi] prince. We are not happy if anyone insults them. Everyone should be sympathetic to them." The Yezidi spiritual council finalized the decision.

"They were forced to [convert]," Baba Sheikh explained during an interview at his home in the town of Sheikhan. He sat on a low sofa and wore white flowing robes and had a long white beard. "If they went with their free will we wouldn't accept them, but they were forced to [convert]."

When the captives escape, they visit Lallish, where they are blessed in the holy spring water under Sheikh Adi's temple as part of a baptism rite adapted for this purpose—proving the malleability of the religion in the light of new circumstances.

"When they come home, the Spiritual Council receives them in Lallish and talks to them. We tell them 'You had to, they forced you, and you will be fine.' We help them psychologically, and have helped send some women to Germany for treatment.

"It is our job to pray for not only women and girls—not only Yezidis but for peace in the whole world," he said, while also criticizing the UN and international community for not doing more to help.

I asked him if he was concerned that Yezidis immigrating to Europe might lose their faith: "People are more religious than before, and the reason why is because they want to fight; they want to keep their religion and their faith and that's why they were resisting the enemy," he said.

The Yezidi religious authorities responded quickly to the enslavement. One night in early autumn 2014, I saw Baba Sheikh counseling a young woman who had just escaped from Fallujah, in Anbar province. She was one of the first to return and he offered her his support and guidance. This meant a great deal to her because of his religious rank, and made her return much easier than it otherwise would have been. Fear of being rejected was one of the main reasons why women and girls in captivity killed themselves. In Iraqi Kurdistan, familial violence toward women and so called "honor" killings are still unfortunately rife, and occur in both Yezidi and Kurdish Muslim communities.

Back in Deir ez-Zor, news reached Zahra that captured Yezidi women had been accepted back by their families. The news was amazing. After that she thought to herself that perhaps it would be all right, that perhaps there was some hope after all, but mixed in with this was the still present fear about how her family would react if she did manage to escape.

When she did, finally, make it home, much later, they told her: "You're not the first or the last; there are many cases like yours."

Zahra was relieved. "I didn't expect that," she said, still looking slightly shocked.

But she was not free yet. Her captor, Abu Adafa, was planning to become a suicide bomber. Before he went through with his mission, he made a will, which was witnessed by four ISIS members. The will said that once he was dead, Zahra would be free to travel as she pleased within the Islamic State. It was his dying wish that she should no longer be enslaved, as long as she wore the black veil and did not forget to pray.

"I am going to heaven," he told her the last time that she saw him alive.

"Wish me luck and forgive me if I hurt you in any way," he added. "God willing you get to go back to your family and see them again."

"Let God forgive you, I am not going to forgive you," she said.

After he left, she felt only relief and happiness: at last, this was her chance to escape.

Chapter 9

"Bucca was their school"

Shakir Abdul Wahab Ahmed Zaater was born in 1984 in Habaniya, a former resort town that sits by the Euphrates River, east of Ramadi. His father, Abdul Wahab, was a peaceable man, a taxi driver and the owner of a small shop. He was given the nickname Wahib. It stuck, and later became his son's *nom de guerre*.

Shakir was ambitious at school; he would always try to outdo his friends to become the best, according to one of his relatives who wishes to remain anonymous. As a teenager, Shakir wore tight jeans and preferred to dress in western fashions and sport a western-style haircut—uncommon in Anbar when he was growing up. He grew up with five brothers and two sisters. He went on to study computer science at Anbar University.

His eldest brother, Amr, worked in construction and owned a small shop. After the US-led invasion of Iraq, Shakir's younger brother Hassan joined Jammat al-Tawhid wal-Jihad, an insurgent group fighting the US occupation that was led by the Jordanian jihadist Abu Musab al-Zarqawi. After sowing terror in his native Jordan, Zarqawi had traveled to Afghanistan, where he attempted to join the jihad there, and then to Iraq.

The group targeted US troops as well as Shia Iraqis and Sunnis who didn't conform to its strict views on Islam. The group joined Al-Qaeda after pledging allegiance to Osama bin Laden in 2004.[80] Zarqawi rose to infamy and was nicknamed the "Sheikh of the Slaughterers" because of his appearances in gruesome beheading videos, most famously personally beheading US civilian Nick Berg in a 2004 video. He was killed in 2006 in a US air strike, which took place in Diyala province, north of Baghdad.

At the age of twenty-one, Shakir was arrested by American forces during a raid of his home in Anbar. He was taken to the American-run Camp Bucca detention center in southern Iraq. The GIs that picked him up had apparently been looking for his brother Hassan. Hassan wasn't home, so they took Shakir instead. Camp Bucca was open for six years and held close to twenty thousand detainees at its peak. New detainees were targets for extremists and the prison became a focal point for radicalization.

Abu Bakr al-Baghdadi, who went on to lead ISIS, arrived at Camp Bucca in 2004.

Mahmood Zaki, thirty-two, from Salahaddin province, was detained by US forces for weapons possession and held in a prison in Tirkit, in Abu Ghraib, and finally in Camp Bucca. Zaki didn't become radicalized, but he remembers the power the extremists had. The prison was full of young men like him who had been picked up in sweeping raids. In the Tikrit prison, known as "the stables," he was beaten and kicked by US soldiers, months before the news of US torture and abuse of Iraqi detainees in Abu Ghraib broke.

In Bucca in 2004, Zaki remembers jihadists coming to the prison and spreading their beliefs, which were more extreme than anything he had heard before. "They start recruiting people by telling them that the way they were practicing [Islam] was wrong."

Bucca was more comfortable than Abu Ghraib; it had wider streets, better food, and the detainees had a little more freedom. But it was overcrowded, and the men, mostly from rural, traditional backgrounds, were angry. Their culture and traditions dictated that if a man's dignity was compromised, he should seek revenge.

Some of the men who met at Bucca would go on to join and run ISIS. After Zarqawi's death, the remnants of Al-Qaeda in Iraq became known as Islamic State in Iraq. In 2013 there was a rupture with the Al-Qaeda leadership and the Al-Qaeda franchise in Syria. After US troops left Iraq and the prison where many jihadists had met was closed, the group became the Islamic State of Iraq and Syria (ISIS).

For ISIS, "Bucca was their school," said Zaki.

It was in this milieu, and still behind bars in early 2006, that the twenty-two-year-old Shakir was approached by jihadists. His brother Hassan had blown himself up at a US checkpoint east of Ramadi, but the jihadists told Shakir that he had been killed by US forces. They began to brainwash him. "They were able to reach him because of his brother's death," said Captain Muhammed al-Fahdiway from the Anbar military intelligence. Fahdiway is from the same tribe as Shakir, and they attended the same high school.

In 2006, he was released and went home to visit his family. It was the last time they were to see each other. Shakir went into hiding in Fallujah and joined an assassination team, gaining a reputation for killing large numbers of Iraqi police officers in the city, according to Captain Fahdiway.

In 2011 Shakir was hiding out in a relative's house in the desert near Fallujah when he was captured again—this time by the Iraqi military. He confessed to his crimes and was transferred to an Iraqi intelligence prison in Baghdad. After only a few months, he managed to bribe his way out with cash, according to Captain Fahdiway.

Free again, he moved back into hiding in the Anbar desert where he joined an ISIS unit aiming to cut off the international road between Baghdad and Amman.

In 2013, he appeared in a propaganda video wearing a large beard, tan-colored kaftan, and black scarf. In the six-minute clip, Shakir stands on the side of the road and flags down three passing trucks, before inspecting their driver ID cards and asking if they are Shia Muslims.

The Syrian men look terrified and tell Shakir that no, they are all Sunnis. He evidently doesn't believe them. He asks them if they are Sunni and tries to establish their religiosity by asking how many bowings should be performed at dawn prayer, and then tells them to get down on the ground by the cab of a truck with its engine running.

Some distance away, off in the desert, a group of ISIS fighters can be seen standing by their cars, looking more like a gang of stray thugs than soldiers. The video cuts back to the foreground, and the drivers are shown from behind as they kneel in the middle of the road next to some wooden posts. Shakir walks behind them with a swagger, points his gun and then fires it into the men's heads and backs. Their bodies keel over into the dust, one by one, in slow motion.

Another ISIS fighter turns to the camera and jeers over the bleeding corpses while gesturing at them with what looks like a sword. "Let Nouri al-Maliki [Iraqi PM], his Shiite followers, and his demons see . . . those who are bragging that they insured the international highway between Baghdad, Amman, and Syria."[81]

"His [Shakir's] face was virtually everywhere on the internet and yet was blurred or covered in the official Islamic State pictures and videos, suggesting there was a degree of jealousy about his rise to stardom," said *Il Foglio* journalist Daniele Raineri, who tracks ISIS propaganda.

Shakir's tribe—the Albu Fahd, part of the Dulaimi tribal confederation, is based in eastern Ramadi and is known for its anti-insurgent and generally pro-government stance. Like many tribal groups, the Albu Fahd didn't support the US occupation or the Shia-led governments that followed, but neither did they, on the whole, agree with the goals of the extremists. Many members of the tribe were killed by Al-Qaeda and, later, ISIS.

It is thought that, around the time of the events portrayed in the video, Shakir's mother, older brother, and sister left for Erbil in the Kurdistan region, and then went on to Turkey, according to his relative and Captain Fahdiway. It is not known exactly why they left or when they returned, but by the holy month of Ramadan, which fell in the summer of 2015, they were back in Anbar.[82]

Albu Fahd tribesmen rejected Shakir and his family—especially after his prominent role in the video. "I endured a lot of beatings just because I'm related to him," one of his relatives told me, insisting he remain anonymous. Families who had lost members to ISIS brutality wanted revenge from the families of ISIS fighters: blood in exchange for blood.

Shakir went on to lead a bombing squad known as the Abu Wahib brigade, in honor of his ISIS nickname. Abu Wahib is the name that Leila would know him by in the final years of his life.

--

Leila had been taken by one of Shakir's brothers to a military base near Ramadi. The city fell to ISIS in spring 2015 after a series of massive suicide attacks on the remaining government forces holed up in the city. Then, one night, Shakir visited her and told her that he had bought her. She was now his property. She protested and said he couldn't "marry" her because she was already married and had a daughter. She pointed at her niece.

Leila remembers Shakir as having pale eyes, fair skin, and lank hair. He was short and overweight, and his beard looked as if it had been died black. He had recently been badly injured, having lost a leg in a 2014 Iraqi Army strike and undergone surgery on his head. His hands were also badly burned.

"He couldn't move his hands without putting cream on them, otherwise they would bleed." Leila said. "The first time I saw him he was using a stick to walk."

Shakir ignored Leila's entreaties and proceeded to rape her.

"After he took my honor away he realized I was still a girl."
He accused her of lying about her virginity, and, as punishment,
sent three ISIS guards to gang rape her. Two of the guards were
from Iraq and one of them was Egyptian.

Following her ordeal, Shakir told Leila that he planned to
sell her niece. He could get $1,500 for her, he said. Fearing the girl
would be taken soon, Leila grabbed her and ran away, heading
out onto the dark, unfamiliar roads. The following morning she
was hauled back to the base, where two of the guards beat her
for almost an hour.

"Once you lied to us and you saw I sent three guards to
you," Shakir told her. "What do you think I will do to you
after you tried to run away?" She told him that she was just
trying to save her niece from the fate she had suffered, but to
no avail.

"She's not your daughter and you don't have the right to
talk about her," he yelled.

The next day, he ordered two foreign fighters, one French,
the other Japanese, to gang rape her. It was the holy month of
Ramadan, and Leila was fasting during daylight hours. After the
attack Leila was in considerable pain and continued to bleed for
the next two weeks.

Leila asked Shakir if she could see a doctor because of the
bleeding, but he told her no, the injury was part of her punishment for trying to run away. At the base he gave her daily

contraceptive pills. When they made her throw up, he switched to giving her contraceptive injections instead.

After Ramadan, he brought Leila to a house in Rutbah, a small town of thirty thousand people in Anbar province, four hundred kilometers west of Baghdad. His family was living just outside the town in the house of his married sister.

Shakir was now the military commander of Rutbah, but that didn't mean he had an influential position in ISIS, explained Hisham al-Hashimi, an adviser to the Iraqi government. "He was not a leader. For ISIS he was one of the field commanders, the third tier command and not close to Baghdadi." Other sources said that Shakir was widely distrusted inside ISIS, and never held any prominent positions in the organization.

"After Ramadan, he took me to a house alone and locked the door. Every couple of days they would bring two or three Yezidi women or girls," Leila told me. Shakir was trafficking the women for sex with men in the area. They returned to Leila after their ordeals, crying about being raped and beaten.

"I thought he was perhaps in love with me," Leila said, because, despite repeatedly attacking her, he never sold her on, despite her frequent requests that he do so. He also didn't rent her out like the other women.

The house where Shakir kept Leila was directly underneath a large telephone mast, and had previously been occupied by a doctor. Shakir came to visit regularly, but he always made sure to lock the door from the outside on his way out. Every few days he or his brother brought food for them. He made Leila sleep in a large double bed, like a marriage bed, she said.

When ISIS achieved a military victory, they forced citizens under their control to go out onto the street and celebrate. At one such gathering, with military vehicles passing and honking their horns, Leila noticed that people seemed scared of Shakir. "I tried to catch the attention of a passing civilian in the hope that they could help me, but they ignored me."

One night, when Shakir was asleep beside her, Leila tried to grab his gun, which was lying next to the bed. Maybe she could shoot him, she thought, and steal the house keys in order to escape back to Sinjar. But as she lunged forward, he raised his hand and grabbed her outstretched arm.

"Do you really think I would sleep like that?" he sneered, shoving her away from the weapon.

The next day he sent her niece to stay with his family, so she was alone when four ISIS fighters from Rutbah came to gang rape her. The men stayed until the morning. "I almost died," she recalled. "I became very bad psychologically and had a fit." She collapsed, just as she had done regularly when she was younger.

When she told Shakir about her illness, he accused her of lying. Eventually he agreed to take her to an Islamic spiritual guide who, he said, would reveal to Shakir if Leila really was unwell. "If you are lying and you don't have this disease then I will do worse than what I have already done," he warned her.

The sage examined her and told Shakir that Leila was indeed sick and that she had clearly been ill for a long time. He said that Shakir would be in trouble with the governor of the area if he found that she was being mistreated and hadn't been taken to see a doctor.

Shakir agreed to take Leila to Mosul to see a doctor. The doctor spoke English and Leila didn't understand him. He gave her two injections and some pills, which stopped the fainting fits.

--

Periodically, Shakir brought Leila to see his family, who lived outside of Rutbah. During these visits, Leila and Shakir would stay next door in a house that formerly belonged to a teacher. His mother was sometimes kind to Leila, and took a shine to her niece, buying her gold earrings and telling Leila that she wanted the girl to marry Shakir's nephew when she was old enough.

Shakir's brother, in contrast, told Leila that she was still an infidel because she kept trying to run away, and that she would only be set free if she truly converted to Islam and read the Koran, at which point she could marry and be a free woman inside the Islamic State.

"I am already praying! Shakir has 'married' me! What else is left for me to become a Muslim?" she asked him.

On one visit after Ramadan, Leila met a tall, skinny, and young woman who came from a nearby village, who, she was told, was Shakir's new wife. Prior to this encounter, the woman was unaware that Shakir had a slave. She took an immediate dislike to Leila when she found out. "I know he comes to you," she hissed at Leila. Shakir tried to convince her that Leila was, in fact, his brother's slave, but she didn't believe him and told him to sell Leila or she would insist on a divorce.

Before he got married, Shakir had visited Leila every night and stayed until morning. Now he came only every other day. Leila was now in constant pain from the repeated assaults she had endured. "He has come to me so often that I am swollen and I cannot walk," she told another Yezidi girl who was staying at the house before being sold on.

Shakir was generally angry and fiercely possessive with Leila. When they were together he would stop her from checking on her niece in the next room. He also forced the young girl to call him father. "Who is your father?" he would ask repeatedly, demanding that she reply, "Abu Wahib."

Chapter 10

"No one can bring back the dead"

In Manbij, after the birth of her child, Nadima asked the ISIS emir if she could work as a servant with his family instead of staying on her own, but he refused. She only got to visit his family later in secret, after a group of female members of ISIS, women she described as "girls of the state," came to visit her and agreed to take her there.

When the time came, they wrapped her top to toe in a black cloak that all women under ISIS are required to wear. Arriving at the house, the ISIS women with Nadima pretended to be there to pass on sewing instructions to the women in the emir's family. Nadima stayed silent—Kurdish is her mother tongue and if the emir's family realized she couldn't speak Arabic, she might have been discovered. Most Sinjari Yezidis understand Arabic to some degree but women who stayed at home and didn't attend school are less likely to be fluent.

A short while later, encouraged by her trip out into Manbij, Nadima tried to escape again. But once outside the apartment she got lost. She was afraid to ask a taxi driver for directions in case he was an ISIS member who would bring her back to the emir. In any event, the emir realized she was gone and soon found her, bringing her back to the apartment.

That evening, he announced he intended to punish her by taking away her three youngest children—a girl, aged five, a boy of eighteen months, and her newborn baby boy who was just over a month old. When he brought them back one hour later, she saw that they were feverish.

The children were throwing up and all of them had high temperatures. Nadima convinced the emir to take them to the hospital, by which time the children were in a dangerous condition. She didn't know what was wrong with them.

The doctor came, but it was too late to save her newborn boy, who died "right there in front of me," she said.

The doctor told her that they had been poisoned. The other two children both died within an hour. "He killed three of my children," she said, becoming frantic with grief again, her eyes filling with tears. She clutched tightly at her wrists with her hands as she spoke. "I was crying; I lost my mind. I tried to kill myself in the hospital so they would put me in a prison."

"Just give me their bodies so at least I can wash them," she begged the nurse, but they had already been washed and put to rest in the hospital's morgue.

"They brought [their bodies] to me in the prison, wrapped up their clothes and laid them on the mattress. For a while I was kissing them and crying and beating myself. After that, they took them away and locked the door. I don't know what happened to them; whether they buried them or threw them away, I have no idea."

--

"After the children died he put me in another apartment near the hospital on the third floor." Again, the door was firmly locked. Even though she repeatedly told him that she was married, he still came to rape her while her one remaining daughter slept in the next room.

One night, to avoid his advances, she pretended to be asleep. He told her to wake up, but she didn't respond, so he dragged her by the arms, pulled her into the bedroom and threatened to sell her if she didn't submit. "I will kill myself or you kill me, but don't rape me," she begged, but he did it anyway. "I couldn't control him," she said bitterly, her lips shaking with anger.

This continued for seven months. Once, while she was ill, he took her back to the hospital and she managed to speak to a nurse who told her she had photographs of her babies, taken before they were buried. The nurse felt sorry for her and agreed to let Nadima use her mobile to call her brother-in-law back in Kurdistan. Nadima told him to organize a feast in honor of her children, because they were dead.

On another of his visits, the emir brought Nadima's daughter a mobile phone to keep her entertained. A long time had passed since her last escape attempt but she never stopped trying. When the emir left, she used the phone to call her brother-in-law again. With his help, she began to plan to run away again. "Don't worry," he told her, "we will send a smuggler to you."

"One morning there was no cooking gas and my daughter was crying with hunger. I looked around and noticed that the apartment's side doors, which had previously been covered by a mosquito net, had been left open." Checking that the coast was clear, Nadima told her daughter to put on dark clothes and get herself ready—this was their chance to escape.

Nadima knew where the nurse lived. She went there and asked her to hide them until they figured out where to go next. The nurse agreed, so she called her brother-in-law and he promised to send a smuggler to pick her up there. However, the house was in a risky area so she had to move on again. When the time came, Nadima put her black veil back on and gave a bag to her daughter to be used as a signal to tell the smuggler who they were. They crept outside onto the streets of Manbij, and walked a little way before two cars approached.

A small Kia van drew up beside her and the driver spoke quickly. "Get in," he said. Nadima and her daughter climbed into the backseat and the car sped off toward the outskirts of the city. They changed cars to make sure they were not being followed, and then traveled back inside Manbij to a house of one of the smugglers. It was during the midday prayer so the streets were quiet. They waited until 4 p.m., the next prayer time, when another man came to transport them to a different safe house. They waited in Manbij for six more days.

"We couldn't go out because everyone was searching for us and we were supposed to be hidden." The owner of the house was an ISIS member, and while he hid Nadima and her daughter, he also pretended to go out searching for them. After a week, when it was safe to travel, he drove them along the main road to Raqqa, just over one hundred kilometers southeast.

As directed by the smuggler, when they arrived in each new ISIS-held town or village, Nadima had to change cars and drivers. The men gave Nadima their wives' ID cards to show at ISIS checkpoints that dotted the road.

"I was very scared during this time. I thought, 'if they capture me again they will take my daughter from me as well and they will do whatever they want with me.'" She was leaving Syria without her husband and four of her five children.

"They took my husband, they killed and captured my children and I am left with only my one daughter," she said. The dark orange earth of northern Syria flashed by the car window under a gray wintery sky.

The journey took a total of ten days and her uncle sold his house to pay the smugglers $10,500. Nadima now lives alongside her family in a camp not far from the Turkish border. She stays alone when she can and prefers not to interact much with her relatives. She spends much of her time thinking about her dead children, her other daughter, who is still with ISIS, and the husband she fell in love with on her parents' farm all those years ago in Kojo.

In August 2016, Manbij was liberated from ISIS by US-backed Kurdish and Arab fighters and there were jubilant scenes of women and girls smiling, laughing, throwing victory signs and lighting up cigarettes. The nurse, and the smugglers who helped her, were likely to have been part of the celebration.

When I went back to visit Nadima in the camp in Iraqi Kurdistan, she was wearing black bracelets embroidered with the names of her children and husband. The only time she smiled was when she recalled passing messages back and forth with Elias before their marriage. "I was happy for a moment when I returned; but still my happiness is not complete because [four of] my children did not come back with me and I don't know anything about Elias."

"They say they did this because we are Yezidis, but we did not choose this religion. Yezidism was there before we were born. This wasn't our fault. . . . Why would they kill children because of religion?" she asked me, sitting in her sparse tent beneath the Mountains. It was raining outside. Later the men of the camp gathered to watch a football match not far from where we were sitting.

Her surviving daughter is now twelve and had just returned from school as we talked. Her long hair was in a fishtail plait, braided by her aunt that morning, after Nadima had given her a shower. She is almost the same age that Nadima was when she met her father.

"I am happy with her but I will never forget her older sister [who is still with ISIS], her father, or the three children they killed. I still don't know where their bodies are. They threw them somewhere, three young children; two boys and a girl. If I die but my daughter survives and her father returns, it would be better than living like this."

She began to cry gently and wiped her eyes with her sleeve. Most female Yezidi survivors have suicidal thoughts, made worse by life in the tightly crammed camps with no way home, nor privacy or a way to earn a living.

Nadima also wore a thin necklace made of braided red and white cotton. She arrived back from Syria in January 2016, just in time for a Yezidi holiday celebrating the end of winter. Her husband's family made the bands, which, she told me, are supposed to bring good luck to the wearer and have holy significance.

Nadima may be free but it is a bitter kind of freedom. She feels ashamed when her daughter asks her to buy something small and she can't afford to. "At least if I could support her things would be better." These feelings are as bad for Nadima as the losses she has suffered in her family.

She's angry and believes that if foreign powers had wanted to rescue the women and children, they could have done so. "There would be no one left, all the kidnapped women would be returned," she says bitterly.

"If anyone comes and asks, I will tell them what happened to me; but no one can bring back the dead."

Part III:
The Accomplice

Chapter 11

"I was a hunter on Sinjar Mountain"

Men stood and stared as a strange new convoy passed on the main street of Hardan, a town to the north of Sinjar Mountain. The pickup trucks, their horns blaring as they sped by, were filled with scruffy young men gripping machine guns. Many of the men wore black t-shirts and khaki trousers. One sported shin pads over his gray tracksuit, with a green scarf slung around his neck. On their feet were the flimsy, dust-covered sandals that are ubiquitous during the summer months. Their hair and beards were only just starting to look overgrown.

But who were they? Perhaps the fighters that everyone had feared? Some looked familiar. A few people on the street raised their hands in acknowledgment or greeting; others just stared or pointed their cell phone cameras at the procession.

On the side of one truck, the villagers could read the words "Islamic State Ninawa Province, Al Jazeera territory, Saifuallah Unit." It was ISIS.

The convoy headed toward the village square, where it came to a halt. A young man, with tousled black hair and a military vest, sat in the back of a flat-bed truck. He swiveled in his seat, turning his mounted machine gun in an arc so it pointed back toward Sinjar Mountain. It was just before midday, and the sun was blazing in the hard, blue sky.

--

Like other towns around the Mountain, Hardan is mostly made up of one-story buildings, except for the two-story school that sits on the eastern edge of the town, and a row of dusty shops. Lying at the end of a small road, it has the feeling of being adrift amid the surrounding yellow plains. On the horizon is the smudge of Sinjar Mountain where thousands had already fled on that morning. On the southern plains below, the killings had already begun.

The Peshmerga pulled out of Hardan at about 10:30 a.m. on August 3, 2014, said Sulaiman Adi, a balding man with a bright smile and quick movements who works for the local KDP office, and enjoys hunting for partridges on Sinjar Mountain and keeping them as pets.

After the Peshmerga left, the Yezidis' Turkmen and Arab neighbors came to tell the Yezidis to raise white flags, which would protect them from ISIS, who were likely to arrive soon. Sulaiman was not sure about this advice. There was something about the way a Sunni man had asked one of his neighbors "Why have *your friends the Peshmerga* fled?" that bothered him. He gathered his family and belongings and headed to the Mountain.

On the way to the Mountain, he got a call from one of his relatives telling him to come back. "We're taking pictures with the ISIS fighters now so it is fine—they're not hurting anyone," the caller said. Sulaiman turned around.

--

When he got back to Hardan, ISIS had already left. The town's generators were running as normal and the people who had crowded into the village streets had now gone home.

It was then, at 2 p.m. in the fake calm of that afternoon, that Sulaiman suddenly heard the village elder shouting "Run for your lives, save yourselves!" People were dashing from their houses into the street, taking flight. News of the massacres that were taking place on the south of the Mountain had now reached Hardan. But it was too late.

The ISIS convoy returned and was blocking the road leading out of the town. Sulaiman's family managed to drive through the junction before the road was severed, but those who came minutes afterward were not so lucky. More than sixty-five Yezidis (probably many more) were captured and killed across five sites. The bodies have yet to be dug up and accounted for.

Sulaiman and his family drove west toward Kurdistan. At the first ISIS checkpoint they were allowed to pass. But in Snuny, the vehicle was stopped and searched for weapons and phones.

His neighbors were gathered near the entrance to the town of Khanasor, on the road to Syria. After sunset, they were instructed to drive in their convoy of twenty-four cars containing families from Hardan and Khanasor west toward Shadadi, across the border.

Along the way, a few cars managed to veer off the road and escape. Their ISIS escorts, armed with machine guns, were in two vehicles at the back and front of the convoy. Sulaiman considered trying to escape, but his brother was in a separate car and he had no way of coordinating with him, so he decided against making a break for it.

When they arrived in Shadadi, hundreds of Yezidi captives were corralled into a village school with the men on the first floor and the women and children on the second. ISIS guards fed them with canned meat, fish, and small pieces of bread. Sulaiman recalls that the guards were in some cases aggressive, including one Tunisian in particular, whilst others were a little kinder: one Iraqi told the other guards not to walk among the Yezidi children with their weapons. When an Egyptian Imam came and instructed them to convert to Islam, they agreed. They had no choice.

The captives were now loaded onto five large tourist buses, which had previously been used to take Iraqi pilgrims to Saudi Arabia. The young men and boys were put on one bus, single women and girls on another, and families in the remaining three. Sulaiman stayed with his wife and children but was separated from his two teenage nephews.

The buses now headed back into Iraq. Sulaiman saw many corpses of Yezidis lying by the highway around Sinjar and became frantic. "I was praying to God that an airplane would come and strike us and kill us all because I didn't want to see anymore."

Near Sinjar the convoy split. The buses filled with men went one way and the rest headed to Tel Afar. But there was no room in any of the schools or prisons there so they continued on. The same thing happened at a military base near Mosul. Eventually, the women and girls ended up in Mosul, and Sulaiman's and the other families were taken to the Qayyarah airbase, south of the city. At the base, they were guarded by tribesmen, who, surprised to see Yezidi prisoners, said they were sure a mistake had been made and that they would soon be free. They took pity on the prisoners and convinced ISIS to allow the families to be reunited with their sons, even offering to act as guards on the way to protect them, under the strict codes of Arab hospitality. A month later, ISIS agreed, and five Jibouri tribesmen accompanied Sulaiman and two hundred Yezidi captives on the journey back to Kojo, where the young men had been sent previously.

Arriving in Kojo, Sulaiman saw dead bodies piled everywhere. He helped in the efforts to bury them. Some of the bodies had been covered with earth using digger trucks, but dogs had still managed to devour some of the remains. In one ditch, he saw about twenty bodies. There were hundreds more at different points around the village, and still more in the school building and on the football field.

Hundreds of captives were being held in the empty houses of people who had been killed or had fled. Sulaiman was told to find an empty house. Once he found one he locked the door and decided to go out only if absolutely necessary. He hoped this would make it less likely for him and his family to be recognized by ISIS if they tried to escape.

Living in the shadows of the dead was ghostly and did strange things to the captives.

"It was a horrible, terrifying situation," Sulaiman said, looking pained. "Sometimes we would hear strange noises in the night and we were scared because we knew they had killed so many innocent people. My friend heard a child crying one night inside a home—but when he went to look, there was no one there."

The men were forced to pray five times a day in the house of the village mukhtar, which had been turned into a mosque after he was killed. The women had to pray at home. "Their main goal was to convert us," Sulaiman said.

Sulaiman's oldest daughters are fourteen and fifteen. Being small and young-looking for their age, Sulaiman and his wife decided to disguise them as boys so they wouldn't be enslaved. "We made them wear t-shirts and dirty clothes and cut their hair short."

In late November 2014, the local ISIS leader, Abu Adnan, was killed when a fight broke out over a failed Yezidi escape attempt. In retaliation, the unmarried women and girls were sent to Syria, and the rest of the hostages—nearly eight hundred Yezidis—were transferred to Tel Afar.

As Sulaiman and his family were driven away, ISIS fighters on the roads shouted out to them, calling them devil worshippers. After the death of the local leader, in winter 2014, the captives were moved to Qasil Qio, a town close to Tel Afar. Here, life was a little calmer. ISIS was now under intense military pressure from coalition air attacks and the fighters mostly ignored their prisoners.

Some Yezidis began working as shepherds for ISIS, using this freedom to sneak away. That December, ISIS brought buses, trucks, and trailers to Qasil Qio and told the hostages that they were going to be moved again. It was Sulaiman's last chance to escape.

He returned home quickly and pulled the closet away from the wall, leaving just enough room to crawl behind it with his wife and six children. They stayed hidden there for almost five hours while ISIS rounded up the other captives. As they waited silently, Sulaiman's son cried out for bread. "Wait until it gets dark," his father whispered to him, urgently.

--

When night fell, Sulaiman crept from the house. He saw no one around. The other captives had already been taken away. The family ran out into the darkness until they came to a small river. The water was cold and the current strong. It was raining. The journey soon proved too arduous for Sulaiman's elderly mother, who couldn't walk any farther. They had no choice but to abandon her.

Beyond the river, they met another Yezidi family who were also escaping. They continued along the dirt roads together, carrying their children, terrified that they would be spotted. Eventually they made it to an empty farm building where they rested through the following day, their hunger hardly sated by eating some tinned tomato paste they found in the house.

That night, they started to move again toward Sinjar Mountain, and by the evening they reached the village of Ayn al-Hisyan. It was freezing cold but the dark provided cover. They slept in a shallow valley, keeping their heads low to avoid being spotted by local shepherds. They stayed there all the next day, too scared to move.

"From the valley we tried to cross the highway but the road was exposed and oncoming cars could see us, so we lay down flat on the embankment." When at last, there was a gap in the traffic, they headed on again, past a small Arab village and Sinjar's cement factory, and finally on toward the Mountain. They used a compass illuminated by a cigarette lighter to guide them in the right direction.

Once in the foothills, Sulaiman kneeled and kissed the ground, praising Melek Tawuse, the peacock angel and the Yezidi God's representative on earth. But his wife said, "We're not safe yet, don't cheer so loudly." She is a calm, young-looking woman. "It doesn't matter if I die here now. I am on Sinjar Mountain," Sulaiman replied.

That night, airplanes flew overhead. The family waved toward them, hopeful that they would be recognized as civilians. The damp air was bitterly cold and Sulaiman decided to burn his brother's coat to keep his children warm. On earlier hunting trips, he had buried bottles of water in the Mountain, and he now went to retrieve them for his family.

It took the family days to reach the summit. By the time they got there it was late December, and the siege of the north side of the Mountain had just been broken. ISIS had been pushed out of Hardan by eight thousand Peshmerga fighters as part of a two-pronged attack that began in the middle of the month. The Peshmerga advanced from Zummar and Rabia, backed up by a blitz of forty-five coalition air strikes. "It was a very big operation and thankfully it was concluded very successfully," said

Masrour Barzani, Chancellor of the Kurdistan Region Security Council and the son of the Kurdistan Region's President Masoud Barzani.[83]

Before the offensive, the only access to Sinjar Mountain had been by helicopter over ISIS-held territory. Now, Hardan and the road to Kurdistan were free, although Sinjar city would remain under ISIS control for almost another year.

When I visited Hardan in May 2016, the grass had grown long by the sides of the streets that ISIS convoys had sped down. The town was destroyed and the bazaar stood in ruins. Only a few families had dared to come back and the Peshmerga stationed there were jumpy. The road into the town was flanked by tall earth berms with small lookout posts covered in graffiti and flags, marking what used to be the front line.

Sulaiman and his family now live in a camp for displaced Yezidis in Iraqi Kurdistan and are hesitant to return to Hardan. His mother was rescued by local Arabs and the Kurdish Asayish force. For a long time after they escaped, his children continued to talk in whispers, unable to overcome the fear from their nightmarish journey to escape.

--

When the hostages were rounded up in Tel Afar, one of Sulaiman's female relatives was taken to Mosul and then sent on to Syria. Amera has thick eyebrows, pale skin, and a quick, low voice. When we met, her hair was covered in a brown, lace scarf. In Syria with her two young children, she was sold as many as three times per day.

Amera tried repeatedly to escape her captor in Mosul. Each time the neighbors heard her, and she was caught. The second time she tried to flee, three men sent by the Kurdish forces to save her were captured and killed. As she recounted this, her cheeks flashed red with anger. "I believe in God. I had faith and I knew I would escape."

She never gave up in her attempts to escape, though she did twice try to end her own life, once by dousing herself and her children in gasoline. Even though she knew it would provoke a violent response, she continued to hurl insults at the men who imprisoned and raped her: "You're not religious, you're criminals," she told them. She was whipped with a hose by the wife of one fighter, and her three-year-old daughter was hung upside down and beaten. Her younger brother was whipped until he bled.

When in Mosul she saw on a Kurdish TV channel that Yezidi women and girls who had been taken as slaves were being accepted back by their community. "It was very, very good to hear that," she said. Sulaiman, sitting nearby, agreed and added that he wished Yezidi in past centuries had received similar treatment. "In the old days they were stupid," his elderly mother joined in. They sat together in a small tent made by sewing together colorful blankets.

In Syria, in the hope that her captor, a Saudi, would let her go, Amera had feigned sickness by making her gums bleed with toothpicks. Eventually he agreed to sell her back to her family for $25,000, as long as she promised not to return to her husband or the Yezidi religion.

He thought she had converted, but at night when she was alone with her children, she taught them about who they really were, about their religion and real family. "I would rather die than forget about my religion," she said.

Sulaiman's family sold a machine gun and borrowed money from neighbors and friends to pay for Amera's ransom. Before Amera left, the Saudi fighter gave her two phone numbers and told her, "If your family isn't good to you, you can call me and come back."

What would she do if she saw the ISIS fighters who held her again? I asked.

"I would eat them," she said.

On one visit to his tent, Sulaiman showed me a video of himself with a live female bird, a kind of partridge that is found on the Mountain, attached to his wrist. The video was taken during spring mating season, and in the background, I could see green, rolling hills. He smiled as he watched himself releasing the bird with a thrust of his wrist. She flew away, low at first and then higher over the grass.

Chapter 12

"If it wasn't for her, I couldn't have done it"

Nergez and her family had become lost on their way to the Mountain in the intense heat of the day. The way Sinjar had fallen without any warning seemed incomprehensible to them; there was just the confusion of bullets hitting the side of her house and then the sight of people and animals fleeing in long lines across the plains.

They were desperately thirsty and the Mountain seemed so vast. They were with a group from the village of Tel Banat and the young and elderly couldn't keep up. Soon they were rounded up by men with guns, and driven like sheep to a large, pink wedding hall at the foot of Sinjar mountain. Thousands of people were already inside, held as prisoners.

The prisoners' names and ages were put into a register by the tribesmen who were guarding them, and they were then transferred to a military base for ten days, before being driven along bumpy, rural roads to Badoush prison. Inside, the cells were so crowded that the prisoners had to sit or stand, unable to lie down. Rumors circulated that ISIS had put drugs into their food. The guards became nervous when airplanes flew overhead.

After forty days inside the prison, Nergez and her five children were bused to a school in Tel Afar. By then, thousands of other Yezidi prisoners had passed through these schools and were being sent on around the caliphate. Girls rubbed ash on their faces to make themselves look unattractive as they were taken away from their families.

In Tel Afar, Nergez's fifteen-year-old daughter was taken away, and a month later, Nergez was moved to the farm in Raqqa where Leila and Zahra had been held. More than two thousand women and girls were now being held there.

After they arrived at the farm, Nergez's fourteen-year-old daughter was spotted by the guards. "She was crying as they grabbed her hair and dragged her away," Nergez told me. She held on tightly to her two small toddlers. Her son was picked out and told he was going to be sent to an ISIS military training camp in Raqqa. Nergez was to go with him.

The base looked like a former school. Its walls were covered in bullet holes. The young boys, a mixture of Yezidis, local

Syrians, and the children of foreign fighters, were given religious and ideological instruction. They had to wear military uniforms and were taught how to fight in a fenced-off courtyard outside the building.

"They were teaching them the Koran but my son didn't know how to read it, so he was beaten in front of me," Nergez said. Her son was fourteen years old and was so scared he began wetting the bed. Nergez recalled that the two ISIS fighters in charge of the training camp were also buying and selling women.

--

Under ISIS rule, Yezidi boys above age seven are taken away from their mothers. They are then taught to use a range of weapons including AK-47s, RPGs, and grenades, and are forced to watch gruesome videos of battles and beheadings. They are instructed to recite the Koran, and to regard their families as infidels. Sunni Arab boys are also trained in this fashion, with the pupils split evenly between local and foreign children.

George is fourteen years old and is a relative of Leila's from Kojo. He is a bright, bashful boy with big brown eyes and dimples. Before the ISIS attack he was the top of his class. After he was captured, along with all the other boys in his school, he was put in an ISIS training base near Raqqa. At first, the boys were scared to fire the weapons, "but we got used to it," he said.

Dr. Taib Nezar, director of health in the city Dohuk, Iraqi Kurdistan, said that not enough attention has been paid to Yezidi boys who were forced to train as fighters. "These boys were exposed to a different kind of torture. They were threatened, armed, and asked to kill people. These are children and they were victims of abuse, whether by brainwashing, or by torture, or by being made to torture others. We have to treat these boys as victims and provide help for them."

As of mid-2016, UNICEF Iraq had identified thirty-seven boys who were forced to fight with ISIS, but many more were being prepared for battle in training camps. Residents in the Mosul suburb of Zuhur, who lived near a former orphanage, said it was used as an ISIS training facility for Yezidi and Shia boys between the ages of three and sixteen. An orphanage worker told Reuters that ISIS taught the Shia boys how to pray and forced the Yezidis to convert.

Groups of children arrived every few weeks from outside Mosul and Syria. Older boys were sent to Tel Afar for more intense military or judicial training. One boy was killed in the battle of Fallujah in the summer of 2016. When the other children heard of his death, they were deeply upset.[84]

Manjie's ten-year-old son "Iyad," was sent to a military camp where ISIS fighters showed him violent videos and dead bodies. "Now he is psychologically unstable. He is always fighting and beating his siblings," she said.

Iyad is small and thin and can't sit still. One day in Syria, when he and his mother were alone together, he became distressed and told her there were four men in the room beating him and telling him to stop praying and wearing the ISIS uniform. "There was no one there. Only he could see them," Manjie said.

At the training camp, an ISIS imam tried to teach him to read the Koran, but Iyad would scream and say that three invisible men were telling him not to study the book.

Manjie kept a small piece of bread that she had baked in Tel Afar with her when she was taken to Syria to be sold with her children. "At each ISIS checkpoint, I kept [the piece of bread] with me and I prayed for it to protect me," she said.

When Hassan felt distressed she placed his hand on her chest over the crust of bread, and prayed to Sheikh Shams and Pir Ali, holy figures in the Yezidi religion, for his nightmares and visions to go away. Pir Ali has a shrine in Lallish and is known for the gift of curing madness and possession by jinns.[85]

In Syria, Iyad became attached to the ISIS fighter who was his guard and cried when he was taken back to Kurdistan. He thought his captor was his father and, when they returned home, he tried to prevent his real father from entering his mom's room at night.

In Raqqa, a twenty-year-old young Yezidi woman was forced to work on an ISIS Improvised Explosive Device (IED) production line, with six other Yezidis. At the factory, her boss was a

Syrian who told her to take the empty shell of a rocket or pipe and fill it with white powder. He told her that, with the bomb making skills she was acquiring, she could go back to Kurdistan and blow up her family.

--

Nergez was forced to leave her eldest son at the base, and was taken to the underground prison in Raqqa with her two toddlers. There, she witnessed the prison guards beating a grief-stricken woman with the butt of a rifle to make her stop crying. When the screech of fighter jets was heard overhead, the guards scattered, locking the doors behind them.

After forty days in the prison, Nergez was sold as a domestic worker to a Tunisian man living in Tel Abayad, near the Turkish border. He forced her to read the Koran and whipped her if she disobeyed him. She cooked, cleaned, and washed for his family and other ISIS men in the area. She didn't mind the work and used it as a way to forget her pain. Her youngest son first learned to talk in the home of the Tunisian. He spoke in Arabic rather than her native Kurdish.

The man's wife was Kurdish and felt sorry for Nergez. She spoke about helping her escape but the plans came to nothing. Instead, Nergez begged the Tunisian man to let her see her kidnapped children again, or to sell her on. He agreed, and he sold her to a man whose nickname was Abu Haffs. He was around sixty, from Saudi Arabia, and lived in Shadadi with his six-teen-year-old wife from Aleppo.

Nergez thought that Abu Haffs was probably responsible for stockpiling war booty collected by ISIS on the battlefield, but he was also trading women. His office was in the center of Shadadi. He had multiple cars and bodyguards, but he spent most of his time at home.

She slept in a room that was also used to store weapons, and once found her four-year-old son playing with a hand grenade as if it were a ball. Strange men regularly came to the house, carrying white plastic sacks stuffed with ammunition for use with the weapons.

More than two hundred Yezidi slaves had passed through the house in Shadadi before she arrived, and the rooms were still crowded with girls. "He would come to the room and pick a girl, and then take her to another room and 'marry' her," she said, using a euphemism for rape. The girls were kept for about a week and then sold on.

Nergez heard that her teenage daughters were also in Shadadi but she had no way of finding them without raising suspicion. Instead, she grew closer to Abu Haff's wife, Alia. Alia tried to stop her husband assaulting the slaves, protesting that they were still virgins.

That summer, Abu Haffs took Nergez and one of her sons to watch a public execution of a man accused of working as a spy.

The man's body was hung up on display in the center of town, and Alia and her husband posed for pictures with the corpse. "I was shaking. I was so afraid," Nergez remembered. He threatened her with the same fate if she did anything wrong.

At home, Nergez cooked for Alia and cleaned the house. The women became close and, consequently, Abu Haffs didn't try to rape Nergez. "She was very good to me," Nergez said. "I helped her and she helped me. I kept her secrets and covered for her when she went out and he came looking for her." Alia was nervous and became angry quickly, but Nergez also saw what seemed like real affection between her and her husband.

Despite their language difficulties, Nergez and Alia talked freely together in the kitchen when Abu Haffs left the house. Nergez did the cooking and Alia played on her phone and called her friends in other parts of Syria and Iraq.

Nergez told Alia the story of what ISIS had done to her family, about her religion and her people. They spoke in a mixture of Arabic and bits of Kurdish, teaching each other words and phrases as they grew closer.

Alia had a rebellious, violent side and once showed Nergez a suicide belt that she said was her own. She teased her husband by refusing to pray and jokingly telling him she was Shia. She told Nergez that she dreamed of becoming a female guerrilla with the PKK. "When we go to their side please help me join them," she said. They were already planning their escape.

Abu Haffs sensed that the women were getting too close. He banned them from talking about the Kurdish fighters or watching the TV, other than the channel that showed endless readings from the Koran.

Alia suspected that Abu Haffs wanted to marry a second wife, so she decided to test his loyalty by hiding and making him search for her. While she was hidden, he began looking, but then became angry with Nergez, accusing her of covering for his wife. Alia reappeared to protect her friend. "This is between me and you, and not her," she said.

Alia's suspicions were soon proved correct. Abu Haffs got married again, this time to a woman from Raqqa. She was younger than Alia, and calmer and patient. Abu Haffs continued to dote on Alia but she was furious and was now set on running away, taking Nergez with her.

Four nights after the new wife arrived, Abu Haffs stayed out until the early hours of the morning. When he got back, he went straight to sleep and the women used this moment to slip on their black veils and creep outside into the first signs of daylight.

They fled with the help of a Kurdish couple whom Alia had met on a visit to the market. Nergez could sense that the smugglers were as terrified as they were. They drove toward the checkpoint at the edge of the town. The Kurdish man told the guard on duty that Nergez was his sister and they managed to get through. She isn't sure how they eventually crossed the

front line, but the smugglers knew the way through the coun-
tryside, and eventually they came to a village on the other side
where they were safe. They stayed there for three nights before
moving on.

When he realized they were missing, Abu Haffs called Alia
on her phone and demanded that they return. "If you come and
get us you can have us," she said, knowing that he would be
unable cross the front line without being killed.

"She helped me escape. If it wasn't for her, I couldn't have
done it," Nergez said.

Together they traveled north toward the Turkish border.
Nergez borrowed money to pay the smugglers. At the border
crossing, the two women said goodbye and Alia slipped away.
Since then they've stayed in touch. Alia wants to come to
Kurdistan to see Nergez again, but she's afraid to do so because
of her ties to ISIS.

Chapter 13

"I see them in my dreams and they are selling me"

"We can't live here," said Zeina, twenty, softly, looking around the abandoned building with plastic walls, where she had been forced to take shelter with her family.

She grew up in Sinjar city and remembers a happy childhood of family trips and picnics. Her father was jobless but her brother was a day laborer. She wasn't able to go to school, but she still dreams that one day she will be able to study. "If you haven't studied, then you are blind," she says.

When she was being held captive in Mosul, her family managed to call her and asked her where she was, but Zeina didn't know—she couldn't read the road names. "If I asked a small child where we were, that child might run and tell ISIS." Now that she is home, she spends her days with her family doing housework. But at night, when she is alone, the fear that she experienced in captivity returns.

Her family were late to escape the ISIS invasion on August 3, and were captured at midday. Zeina was taken almost immediately to a mosque in Baaj, and by 6:30 p.m., she had been loaded onto one of four buses filled with Yezidi girls, and was heading to the Galaxy Hall in Mosul. The women with children stayed in the hall, while the younger girls were taken to a large house nearby where ISIS fighters came to take their pick. There were around forty women there and the most beautiful were soon taken away by men who had previously seized their towns.

Zeina was now sent to the farm in Raqqa, where every night ISIS men came and chose the girls, "as if they were buying vehicles," she said. They were terrified and began planning to escape, searching the ground for anything they could use to unlock the doors of the rooms where they were held.

Zeina wondered if drugs were being secretly put into their food or water; they constantly felt sleepy. Zeina and her cousin were bought by an old man living in Shadadi, where they were kept with many other girls. It's not clear if it was the same house where Nergez was held. They were locked up in a small room and were given just one meal a day. When the girls refused to wash they were shoved into the bathroom, where they were forced to strip and were whipped.

After ten days, Zeina was sold to an Iraqi man who tried to rape her. His wife became angry and lashed out at Zeina. She told the woman that she hadn't chosen to be there, that she had been taken by force, but it made no difference. Such mistreatment of women by other women was not uncommon: a number of women living under Islamic State rule joined the morality police and took part in the punishment of girls for perceived "un-Islamic behavior," such as not covering their faces or ankles.

"After ten days of suffering he gave me to another man as a gift," Zeina said. Her new owner was an Iraqi fighter living in Shadadi. After a week, she ran away and asked the neighbors for help, but they took her back to her captor, who starved her for three days and beat her so badly that she was covered in bruises.

He then sold her to a Libyan fighter known as Abu Zubar who lived in a compound near Deir ez-Zor. There, he locked her in his cabin where the only light came through one small window and she was not allowed to see anyone else. He gave her pills that made her feel constantly tired. She was tied down by the wrists and he tried to rape her repeatedly.

She endured this for two months, barely managing to survive, before she was sold, yet again, to a Libyan fighter known as Abu Baraa. He took her to an apartment in a small Syrian village. Again, her hands were tied, he gave her pills, and repeatedly attempted to rape her. She didn't want to wash, but he made her do so. He forced her to wear makeup and revealing clothes for him.

"You are Yezidi so it doesn't matter what we do with you," he said. For him, the Yezidis were not human.

He tortured her every night for seven months and then sold her to a Syrian fighter whose nom de guerre was Abu Khalid. Now she was moved to a large house containing numerous ISIS fighters in al-Bab, a town located in Aleppo province where she stayed for three months. Abu Khalid raped her every night, and in the day she had to wash dishes and the fighters' clothes.

On one occasion, she discovered the door to her room had been left unlocked. She ran out of the house and knocked on the door of a local family. But they were too scared to help her. "We can't rescue you; if we do they will take our girls," she was told. She had to return to Abu Khalid, who then sold her to an Iraqi fighter living near Sinjar.

He drove her away from al-Bab at night, crossing back through Raqqa along the highway. By morning they arrived in Iraq, where she was held in a house with four other Yezidi girls. They had experienced the same traumas as she had and they comforted each other. "In Syria, I didn't see any other Yezidis; I was always with fighters. So when I saw these girls I was very happy," she said.

In Syria, Zeina was given daily contraceptive pills but in Iraq, hospital staff gave her a contraceptive injection that she was told would last for one month. The other girls in the house had been given the same treatment.

One morning, the fighters went out, leaving the door unlocked, and the girls escaped, running as fast as they could toward the town of Qabusi. Once there, they asked the local Sunni residents to help them, but, Zeina recalled, the villagers only laughed at them and returned them directly to ISIS.

Zeina and her new friends were separated. That was the last time she saw them. The fighters took her to their leader in Baaj; Zeina remembers that his name was Abu Omar. He gang raped her with three other men as punishment. "I just lay down and I didn't see anyone else. I didn't know if anyone else came to me," she said, describing losing consciousness.

--

After this assault, Zeina was sold yet again, this time to an Iraqi fighter. She went to live with his family in Mosul. The man's wife knew that her husband was raping Zeina, and so also treated her badly and made her clean the house. While she lived with them, Zeina pretended to pray and read the Koran, "but in my heart I remained Yezidi."

Eventually, her captor agreed to sell her back to her family for $2,000. Zeina left Mosul on December 13, 2015, nearly a year and a half after she was kidnapped. The sky was clear but it was freezing cold when she arrived in the middle of the Yezidi winter festival, known as "Feast for God," during which the faithful fast for three days from sunrise until sunset.

On that morning, the man who sold her to her family drove her away from Mosul to a village near the Peshmerga front line. There she waited for a smuggler to take her across. She had to wade through a river to reach the other side where the Peshmerga fighters were expecting her. "When I saw the Peshmerga position, I felt that I was home."

"Is it all over?" she asked the smuggler. He said she was now with the Peshmerga, and turned and walked back into the Islamic State.

At five that evening, soon after Zeina's escape, ISIS began attacking the Peshmerga front line. She thought that she was going to be recaptured but she was already so desolate that the thought did not frighten her. "I was not afraid of them. I thought that even if they capture me again it's fine—let them kill me. . . . I've suffered a lot. Every day they were beating me lots and I was in terrible pain. After one or two days, I couldn't feel my body. It was like I was unable to move—this happened to lots of girls, not just me," she said. She survived by holding on to the belief that God would help her.

The Peshmerga fighters were kind. They gave her fresh clothes and helped her get warm. The next day they returned her to her family, who had escaped soon after they were captured by ISIS, and now lived in a half-constructed building near Dohuk.

"I never thought I would see them again. I was very happy. My house was full of people. They were waiting for me and they cried and I cried," Zeina said.

She was worried that people would gossip about her and so, at first, didn't want to go to the doctor. She claims not to have any psychological problems, but admits "I'm very angry when I think about them. I get mad, crazy. Many times I see them in my dreams and they are selling me. When I was there I thought, I just want to see my family again once. Now I thank God."

When she returned, she went to Lallish to be blessed in the holy spring. This rite offers comfort to Yezidis, returning them to their faith after they've been forced to convert. Now Zeina largely stays at home, cooking and cleaning. and sometimes visiting her uncle's family. She still hasn't told her family what happened to her in any detail. She says she couldn't live in Sinjar or trust her Muslim neighbors again.

Dr. Nagham Nawzat is a Yezidi gynecologist who has treated over eight hundred female Yezidi survivors. She reports that 90 percent of her patients were raped and most now suffer from depression and psychological problems, exacerbated by the fact that many now live in camps that resemble prisons, surrounded by fences with no privacy and little hope for the future.

In addition to suffering from PTSD, her patients have pelvic infections, irregular periods, and urinary tract infections, as a result of the sexual assaults and filthy living conditions. The women arrive at her clinic emaciated, and often have anemia and skin diseases such as scabies and leishmaniasis, which is spread by sand fly bites and causes large red lesions on the skin.

Zeina doesn't want to get married, and says no one would accept her anyway. In Yezidi culture, as in much of the Middle East, a man's honor is linked to the chastity of his close female relatives. Rape brings shame and suffering to the whole community, which is one reason why it is used as a weapon of war in male-dominated cultures.

The decree issued by the Yezidi spiritual leader, Baba Sheikh, has helped woman reintegrate into society. But the shame and anger is still there. "Our honor is in their hands," said Raed, a twenty-one-year-old student from Siba Sheikheder, one spring afternoon in 2016. "When people take our women and girls it means they take our honor, and we lose the most valuable and precious thing a human being has; this is honor and there is no solution for this. It is just like death—when it is gone, it is gone.

"I wish the number of dead men had been double if only they didn't take our women. We don't care about money and things, we just want our women to come back." Raed told me the story of a man from Kojo who killed himself because of "honor and family . . . it was a dead-end road for him. Out of thirty people [in his family] only one escaped. How was he going to survive?"

In Yezidi communities, as in Iraq and much of the Middle East, the stakes of honor are high. In April 2007 in the town of Bashiqa, Nineveh province, Dua Khalil Aswad, a seventeen-year-old Yezidi, was stoned to death in public by members of the local Yezidi community because, reportedly, she had converted to Islam to run away with a local Sunni Muslim boy. The incident was filmed on mobile phones and seriously worsened tensions between the Yezidi and Sunnis (both Arab and Kurd). In the wake of the killing, there were revenge attacks against the Yezidis. Yezidis from Mosul University were forced to flee and twenty-three Yezidi workers were ordered off a bus and shot in Mosul. Some believe that the 2007 truck bombs killing hundreds that summer in Siba Sheikheder and Tel Azer were carried out in revenge for Dua's murder.[86]

Ido Babasheikh, the brother of Yezidi religious leader Baba Sheikh, said, "Of course [Dua's killing] was a very great mistake and all of us at that time wrote against it, but this is a problem in all of Kurdistan and Iraq, especially Kurdistan. Perhaps every day they kill one like Dua and no one speaks [about it], no one sees it."[87]

Cases of honor killings often go unreported in Iraqi Kurdistan, and estimates of 50-60 females annually killed by their families over honor are probably too low. The killings are also prevalent in the rest of Iraq, the Middle East, and countries across the world.[88]

"Baba Sheikh is in a holy position so the women are more comfortable now. If it wasn't for Baba Sheikh they would rather have died, and it's been useful even for the men," Raed said. At this point Raed's father entered the room and joined the conversation. "The women were forced so Baba Sheikh decided to bless them and accept them back," he told me, adding emphatically, "Now everything is normal in every way."

Chapter 14

"I belong to ISIS and my family are infidels"

In Deir ez-Zor, Zahra now had the letter granting her freedom that she had been given by Abu Adafa, the young Libyan fighter who had blown himself up. With it, she could travel freely inside the caliphate. She decided to go to Tel Afar, where her aunt was in captivity.

While she was there, a number of Yezidis who had escaped were recounting their experiences in captivity on television. This angered ISIS and made it harder for the remaining captives to flee.

During the spring of 2015, ISIS in Tel Afar abandoned their experiment of converting the Yezidis to Islam. The women and children were rounded up and sent to Syria. At the same time an estimated six hundred Yezidi men vanished, and were presumably murdered although their bodies have yet to be found.

Zahra was one of more than five hundred Yezidi women and girls who now traveled across the border from Iraq. But instead of going again to the farm in Raqqa, or to one of the underground prisons in Mosul, she was taken to an ISIS guesthouse not far from the Turkish border. It was here that foreign ISIS women were sent to stay after they had crossed into Syria.

Female recruits stayed in the house with Zahra while their husbands went off to training camps. For single women, the only way out of the guest house was to marry an ISIS member, or to re-marry if their first husband had been killed. The women Zahra met there were from Germany, Canada, the UK, and many other countries.

They studied the Koran every evening, and all day on Sundays and Mondays. ISIS brides from Egypt and Morocco came to give them lessons in Islamic law. Zahra knew a little bit of Arabic but it was hard to converse with the new arrivals who spoke a variety of foreign languages. When she explained why she was there they told her they felt sorry for her and some even admitted to regretting having joined ISIS. "[The new recruits] didn't know what was going on inside the Islamic State or that we'd been forced to convert and marry," Zahra recalled.

Limited Arabic meant that the Yezidi women couldn't always identify the nationality of their captors from their accents, and instead had to rely on what the men chose to reveal about themselves. This made even harder the job of crime investigators who were trying to track down those responsible for trafficking Yezidi women.

After six months in the guest house, Zahra was sent to a house in Raqqa belonging to three Arabic-speaking ISIS members who ran an office registering new recruits and marriages being held in the state. Eighteen other Yezidis were staying in the house with Zahra, including one of her cousins who was working as a servant for an ISIS official. He had been brainwashed by ISIS to the extent that he could no longer remember his previous life. Zahra tried to remind him who he was before ISIS had taken him:

> "You are [name redacted], you are from my village,"
> she told him.
> "No," he responded, "I belong to ISIS and my family
> are infidels. If I see them I will kill them."

When Zahra and the other hostages began plotting their escape, they had to keep the plan secret from him. Zahra understood the way he had been programmed: "Imagine you are a young boy or girl. After two years [of ISIS indoctrination] you will forget about the rituals of your religion. You are scared, you don't understand what is happening, and I come and threaten to kill you and beat you. You will do whatever I want."

Zahra was put under pressure to marry an ISIS member now that she was no longer a slave, but she refused. "I had been through a lot already. I couldn't take anymore."

Because of Zahra's relative freedom, she could visit an internet cafe in Raqqa, where she contacted the smugglers in Kurdistan, who sent her money to buy a phone. The plan was set and, at noon on the agreed day, a woman came to the house where the Yezidis were staying. She introduced herself as a friend of the smuggler.

They followed the woman on foot and were driven to a safe house outside the city where they waited for six days. From there, the smugglers moved them between villages until they came to the front line at Rojava, which was protected by the YPG. The smuggler raised his scarf and waved at the fighters on the other side. He told the captives to run forward toward them.

They were free.

When she finally arrived back to her extended family, Zahra was so tired that she collapsed. They told her that her immediate family were all dead or missing. Today, living in the refugee camp where I met her, she says she can't stop thinking about them.

"I don't think about anything except for my mother, brothers, and my brother's wife. It's been two years and all I do is think about them. I have lost all my other memories. I still don't know what happened to them, especially my brother, who got married less than a year before ISIS came. It is very difficult."

When I left, she wrapped up her face with a scarf so that only her eyes were showing. She headed out into the camp, looking brave but fragile, both old and young, all at the same time.

--

When Shakir Wahib brought Yezidis to the house, Leila asked them if they'd seen any other Yezidi girls. "How were they?" she inquired. The women told her their stories and she realized how similar they were to hers. They could do nothing but cry together.

The months came and went in captivity for Leila. She had been locked away in the house in Rutbah for what felt like a year when, one day in early 2016, Shakir told her that another Yezidi girl was coming to stay for ten days. Leila opened the door, expecting to see a stranger, but it was her sister-in-law. "Wait, let's bring your children inside, too," she said.

"What children are you talking about?" her sister-in-law replied, "I have no children left."

She went on to tell Leila that ISIS fighters in Fallujah had hung her eight-year-old daughter out of the window because she wouldn't stop crying. The girl had subsequently died. Her other two children had been taken away. "She showed me her body and it was all bruised. There were marks from wooden sticks," said Leila. They stayed together for ten days, before the woman was transferred to the town of Hit, also in Anbar province.

Driven by the fear that her niece would be taken away, too, Leila decided that, however dangerous it was, she had to try to escape. Every couple of days Shakir's brother would come and bring food for them, and on one occasion she noticed that he was carrying a bunch of keys. She managed to steal one of them and hid it. Later, she tried the key in the lock on the kitchen door and found it worked. When the brother returned he asked her about the missing key. "What business do I have with your keys?" she asked, feigning indignation.

Leila hid the key under the freezer for the next three months. One day, Shakir brought another Yezidi woman to stay in the house. Leila remembered her from the farm in Raqqa from where they'd traveled to Iraq together. Since then, she'd been moved constantly around Anbar from house to house. In one house, she found a mobile phone and kept it, thinking it might be useful later. When they were alone, Leila grabbed the phone from her.

"I knew that that evening Shakir would come, so I put the phone under the freezer with the key. . . . If he'd found it he would've beheaded us." That night, he checked their bags but didn't find anything suspicious.

Leila called her brother in Kurdistan and told him he needed to send someone to rescue them right away or the other woman would be moved on again, along with the phone, the only way she could communicate with the outside world.

For two days, calls went back and forth between Leila and a smuggler called Abdullah. Abdullah used to work in Aleppo and had a wide network of business contacts in Syria and Iraq. He had become a smuggler after fifty members of his family were kidnapped by ISIS.

Most of the smugglers working to rescue Yezidi women are Yezidi businessmen. Some of the women are bought back from the ISIS fighters holding them, or from the slave markets or online auctions.

The KRG's Office of Kidnap Affairs has repaid the money some families have spent rescuing their girls, but even those receiving such support complain that, often, they have been reimbursed too slowly, leaving them with huge debts. The cost of smuggling is reflective of the danger involved. It's not clear how much of the cash ends up with ISIS, and how much goes to middlemen or the smugglers.

This black market thrives because families are left with no other options. The war against ISIS continues to win back territory from the militants at the time of writing, but there's been no concerted, large-scale effort by local or international powers to rescue Yezidi prisoners.

--

Abdullah sent one of his men to Rutbah to find Leila, her niece, and the other Yezidi woman. At the agreed time, Leila switched the house lights on and off to signal that they were alone. With an air strike nearby causing a diversion, two local women arrived and knocked on the door. Leila opened it cautiously, using the stolen key. "I was very scared and thought it might not be them." The women told Leila not to be afraid and beckoned her to follow them.

The group of women walked through the streets until they reached the smuggler's pickup. They drove quickly away. The smuggler told Leila's friend to act like his wife as they passed the ISIS checkpoints. Leila pretended to be his daughter while the female smugglers acted as sick relatives.

The smuggler drove to his house near Rutbah, where they spent the night. In the morning, they climbed back into the pickup with the children in the front and the women covered in the back. By dusk they had reached the open desert where they were looked after during the night by a shepherd. The following day they left before sunrise and by late afternoon were close to the Iraqi Army lines.

The smuggler here said goodbye to them and left the women standing on the outskirts of a village. It was too dangerous for him to be seen, even by another smuggler. Shortly afterward another man drove up and told the women to get into his car. Leila was anxious and refused to get into the car before she called Abdullah. He reassured her that the man was who he said he was.

They stayed the night in a nearby town before traveling on to the front line. There, they were greeted by Iraqi soldiers who evidently had been expecting them, having received their names from the smugglers. They drove on to Baghdad where they stayed for eight days and Leila was questioned by military intelligence officers about her captivity and escape.

Leila also met with the KDP's Vian Dakhil, who is the only Yezidi member in the Iraqi parliament, and who campaigns internationally on behalf of Yezidi survivors. Dakhil recalled the meeting. "She was crying with me. When we met we cried together for half an hour."

"I was still shocked and traumatized," Leila explained. "I saw Shakir Wahib do a lot of terrible things—actions against God."

From Baghdad, the women traveled north by plane to the Kurdish city of Sulaimaniyah, and then by road to the camps where their families were waiting. When Leila arrived, she collapsed sobbing into the arms of her female relatives. She was in such a state of shock that, for the first few weeks, she had trouble understanding what her family were saying when they tried to talk to her.

"Sometimes I watch the TV and I see the news of the army taking more land and villages, but it's not this that we are worried about—it is our people still imprisoned. We know most of them are in Raqqa, so why are [the army] not going to save them there? Why are they taking these empty villages?" Leila asked me.

Just over a month after her escape, life in the camp was returning to what would have to pass for normality, when the Pentagon announced that Shakir had been killed by an air strike near Rutbah.[89] Shakir was hit in early May near the town's cemetery with three other jihadists, after his movements had been tracked by the Iraqi security forces.

"There was no eulogizing video after his death or campaign of attacks dedicated to him that often happens with the death of prominent [ISIS] leaders," said reporter Daniele Raineri.

During the announcement of his death, the Pentagon mistakenly described him as "ISIL's military [emir] for Anbar Province," giving Shakir a posthumous promotion.

Shortly after he was killed, I went to visit Leila again. The tent in which I found her was filled with members of her family, mostly women, who were chatting in the background. From the corner of the tent blared out triumphal news of battles elsewhere in Iraq. Neighbors were arriving to greet Leila's fourteen-year-old male cousin, George, just as they had done for her, months before. George had just escaped from Raqqa and the mood was buoyant.

I inquired if Leila had heard the news about Shakir Wahib's death. She nodded and smiled and with a calm, satisfied expression, over the chatter in the background, she nodded and said: "I was very happy."

Epilogue

It was a bitterly cold night in early November 2015, more than a year after Sinjar was taken by ISIS. We were camped out in one of the valleys behind the town, close to where Ali had fled with his family, near the ruins of a Yezidi shrine.

At 6:30 a.m., we woke to the pounding thud of bombs hitting the last hideouts of the jihadists in the town. The air strikes had begun just before midnight and picked up pace during the early hours of the morning. Outside the car where I slept, men from the Kurdish Peshmerga's Special Forces units were gathered around bonfires, boiling tea in metal pots and eating steaming bowls of lentil broth for breakfast. The hills were still burnt orange-brown from the summer heat and the sky later that day would be a brilliant blue, a break from weeks of clouds and fog.

When the sun rose, the convoy of seven thousand Peshmerga fighters set off, moving slowly down the tracks of the Mountain where thousands of Yezidis fled in the opposite direction two summers ago. The roadsides were littered with explosives. We were told not to step far away from the convoy even though a mine-clearing team had already swept the road ahead.

At the foot of the valley, where it flattens out onto the plain, the commander called the trucks to halt while the tanks went ahead. A car bomb came hurtling toward the line of men but was hit by Peshmerga fire and exploded before it could get close. A cloud of smoke mushroomed up from the plain. On the hill behind us were US army advisers from the coalition. They were calling in the air strikes that would scatter or obliterate ISIS. They would also level most of the city, fueling the anger of residents who were unable to return to homes that no longer existed.

Exiting the foothills, our convoy reached the Mosul–Raqqa highway but a traffic jam of military vehicles meant that progress was slow. The night before, driving through the Mountain toward the front with the Peshmerga, Yezidis living in tents called out "Apo! Apo!" in honor of the PKK leader Öcalan. Many Yezidis still support the guerrilla group that helped them in 2014.

The seven thousand Peshmerga fighters now moving toward Sinjar needed to win back the trust of Yezidis angry at what they saw as a betrayal when they had withdrawn that August. "For the KDP, the only way to regain popularity is to retake Sinjar," said an anonymous senior KRG political insider.[90] Sinjar is still disputed between Erbil and Baghdad, and the KDP control over the city relies on Yezidi support. Losing popularity to the PKK is a serious threat.

Support for the PKK among displaced Yezidis living on Sinjar Mountain is partly genuine and partly a result of indoctrination. Across the Mountain are graves of the group's martyrs and portraits and graffiti in honor of Öcalan. But the group are also guilty of recruiting children to fight. In early 2015, I met veteran PKK female fighters from Iraq and Turkey, who were training teenage Yezidi girls how to use sniper rifles and other weapons in abandoned buildings on the Mountain.

At the end of 2014, the Peshmerga had recaptured an extensive piece of land stretching up to northern Sinjar. The Mountain then became accessible by road, which made life a little easier for Yezidis who had remained, and meant a small trickle of people could go back to the north side of the Mountain.

Throughout 2015, the front line had remained in Sinjar city, which was mostly controlled by ISIS. The Peshmerga and ISIS engaged in battle around an old water tower on a hill overlooking the old town. Hundreds of Peshmerga fighters were killed and injured here. The Peshmerga have lost 1,600 fighters across Kurdistan since the war began, with nine thousand injured.

In the wake of the ISIS attacks, more than one million displaced Iraqis took shelter in Kurdistan, where many still live in camps and temporary shelters. By September 2014, 465,000 displaced people from Nineveh were living in Dohuk governorate alone, which almost doubled the area's population. Up to 354,000 Yezidis remain displaced in Dohuk.[91] This has placed massive strain on the KRG's resources and infrastructure.

By nightfall, the Peshmerga convoy I was with reached the edge of the city. They advanced and spread out toward an old Iraqi army barracks. Another group of Peshmerga stopped by the southeast of the city as the light faded. They didn't know it at the time but they had stopped at the site of a mass grave that had been covered over with earth.

It was growing dark and so, with a small group of reporters, I went back up one of the dirt roads toward the Mountain. On the outskirts of the city, we stopped at a house with a partially collapsed roof. There, in its ruins, we found a group of young PKK and Yezidi fighters, milling around excitedly. Some of them were only teenagers.

The walls of the house were decorated with brightly colored crayon drawings of AK-47s and paeans to martyrdom. Amidst the rubble in the backyard was the corpse of an ISIS fighter who presumably had been the building's previous occupant. His body lay facedown, frozen in the position of diving for cover, or perhaps having been flung from the building by the force of the same blast that had destroyed the house.

Upstairs, hunched down on the roof, I found a PKK commander, Dilshir Hakoon, one of the early group of PKK fighters who traveled to Sinjar, peering through binoculars toward the city. He barely looked over when I spoke to him, so engrossed was he in his surveillance. He said his troops were giving their coordinates through intermediaries to the US-led coalition to make sure they weren't hit by stray bombing. The PKK had been fighting in pockets inside the city for months and the atmosphere between them and the Peshmerga was tense. The Peshmerga didn't want the PKK to be involved in the fight to retake Sinjar, fearing the group's popularity among Yezidis. While he looked through his binoculars, another car bomb exploded at the edge of the city.

--

ISIS is today losing its hold of some of its territory across Syria and Iraq and is shifting back to insurgent tactics. Sinjar was taken from it in November 2015, the day after the Peshmerga convoy swept down the Mountain. Now the Peshmerga- and PKK-aligned groups observe a hostile standoff, with each force providing arms, training, and patronage to local Yezidis. Brightly colored flags of the various groups flutter above their respective checkpoints, which are sometimes only meters apart along roads that were recently controlled by ISIS.

Thousands of Yezidis have joined the ranks of the Peshmerga, and the KRG also has its Asayish force in Sinjar. The PKK have their own local affiliate called the YBS (Shingal Resistance Units), although its ranks are bolstered with many non-Yezidi fighters, too. The Iraqi police are present, as are the Peshmerga Rojava—a force of Syrian Kurds set up by the KDP as a counterbalance to the PKK.

In early March 2017, a fight broke out between the Peshmerga Rojava and the YBS over access to the town of Khanasor, which has been held by the PKK-linked fighters since late 2014. Control of Khanasor determined who had access to the land corridor to Rojava.

Yezidis who had returned home to Khanasor fled in fear once again. Control of Sinjar is contested by Erbil and Baghdad (the Iraqi government has been paying the salaries of some YBS fighters), but also by the PKK and Turkey who are at war and who both have proxies in Sinjar. Turkey is a close ally of the KDP and supports the Peshmerga Rojava in efforts to oust the PKK.

Erbil-Baghdad tensions have flared in recent years as disputes over oil revenue saw the central government cut the KRG's budget. Kurdistan was plunged into a financial crisis, worsened by a drop in global oil prices and the cost of the war. Teachers and municipal workers, as well as Peshmerga fighters, have gone for months without salaries and strikes have ground public services to a halt.

Yezidis now fear renewed attacks not just from ISIS but also from their Kurdish liberators. Yezidis themselves are not politically homogenous, and many distrust both the Peshmerga as Sunni Muslims, and the PKK because their radical leftist ideology is seen as foreign.

By May 2016, despite the liberation, only 3,220 families had returned to Sinjar district.[92] "It's like a football match," said one Yezidi fighter living in a tent on the Mountain, referring to the political and military competition for control of Sinjar city.

"The KDP want to kick us out of all of Kurdistan," said Egid Civian, the head of the PKK on Sinjar Mountain and a seasoned guerrilla. "We didn't come here with the permission of KDP and we won't leave with their permission, either."

There is a local Yezidi militia in Sinjar, the HPE (Êzîdxan Protection Force), but its influence is limited because of the strength of the Kurdish parties. The group's leader, Hayder Shesho, was temporarily detained by the KDP in early 2015 to prevent him from working with Baghdad, and to pressure him to put his force under the control of the Peshmerga.

"I think after the liberation of Sinjar the PKK will go back to Syria. They should go back because Sinjar is not a second Qandil," said Yezidi and Iraqi MP for the KDP, Vian Dakhil, referring to the PKK's existing base in the northeast of Iraqi Kurdistan. The Turkish Deputy Prime Minister also said they would not allow new Qandil to emerge in Sinjar.[93]

Major General Aziz Waisi took a harder line when I asked him in mid-2016 if the Peshmerga would fight the PKK to force them to leave Sinjar. "Yes. If there is no other way, then we have to—how long can we bear this? . . . They are coming and interfering in our business."

Starting in the spring of 2016, KDP restrictions became tighter on goods and people traveling through the Fish Khabour checkpoint on the road from Kurdistan to Sinjar. The border crossing to Rojava was also closed. This stopped goods and people reaching the PKK-aligned fighters in both Sinjar and in Syria. Turkey is alarmed by the PKK statelet in Syria on its southern border, which is supported militarily by strikes from the US-led coalition.

This impasse is a serious and ongoing impediment to any rebuilding and reconciliation in Sinjar.

Aid convoys delivering goods to Sinjar district have been stopped and turned back by the KDP guards. Trucks full of medicine, food, fuel, and building materials have all been denied access. As a result, food prices have shot up and pharmacies are low on medicine. The lack of building materials getting in (as well as lack of outside support to pay for rebuilding efforts) means many buildings, and nearly all of Sinjar city, remain ruined.[94]

"It affects us and the families, kids, milk, cement, food . . . they even make it hard for us to go and come back," said Fakir

Hasso, an official with the HPE militia, whose men took part in the defense of the Mountain. He called for international protection and self-defense for Sinjar's people as the only solution to the deadlock. Yezidis who are associated with the PKK or aligned groups are regularly hassled in KRG camps by the security forces.

"The determination of rival forces to weaken each other makes the nominal local coalition against [ISIS] weaker," wrote Christine van den Toorn, director of the Institute of Regional and International Studies at the American University of Iraq. "The limiting of resources has created more tensions between forces, as well as more lawless and dangerous activities. Smuggling, in particular, is on the rise, leading to more violence."[95]

While the infighting goes on, ISIS stands only to gain. Yezidis are stuck in a complex series of client-patron relationships with Kurdish leaders where ethnic identification is used in exchange for promises of safety. Meanwhile, the Yezidis remain unable to define their future militarily or politically, as many, if not most, would prefer. While military clashes continue, any political settlement to the rivalry between liberating forces looks a long way off.

As well as leaving explosives buried in the ground, ISIS has also left a landscape of fear and revenge across the places in Iraq it has controlled, which will divide communities further. In early 2015, twenty-one Sunni Muslim villagers were killed by armed Yezidis in revenge for ISIS crimes.

"For every action there is a reaction," an Arab man from Sinjar told Reuters. "This is not over."[96]

--

"Even if we marry or fall in love there will still be this thing inside that is broken," said Leila, reflecting on life after enslavement. Sometimes the women who were taken and then returned are looked down upon because of what they've been through, despite Baba Sheikh's decree. "This is wrong," Leila said. "They didn't go with their own will. They shouldn't do that to them . . . I would fight back."

I was reminded of when Zeina said she thought that no one would agree to marry her now, and about how Raed, the student, who described the loss of honor as being like death. The Yezidis have brought their women, girls, and children back into the community but this doesn't make the pain disappear. Some Yezidi children are fighting on the front line where they may be killed as ISIS loses its territory or hit with air strikes because they are indistinguishable from the fighters around them. Even if they make it home, there are the challenges of de-radicalization.

For some, acceptance comes at the cost of not talking about what happened, even to close friends and relatives. Girls were sent for operations to reinstate their virginity and some abortions were performed in secret for those that returned pregnant.

Surviving is a fight, mentally and physically. Dr. Haitham Abdulrazak, a psychiatrist who worked in a hospital in Zakho, told me about a girl who had run away from Sinjar and come to visit his office with her fiancé. Her family were missing and she felt suicidal. She was diagnosed with post-traumatic stress disorder. Her fiancé was kind and helped her to cope. "When she felt stressed or upset he would bring his mobile phone and make her listen to beautiful songs, love songs. He told her it would all be okay," the doctor related.

"I will marry you very soon," the woman's fiancé told her. Dr. Abdulrazak prescribed antidepressants and she continued to visit him until her condition improved. The couple ran away to Turkey to start a new life together, and before they left in mid-September 2014, they came to his clinic to say goodbye.

Jan Kizilhan, a German-Yezidi professor of psychotherapy, described how his patients from Iraq respond well to narrative therapy after trauma, because storytelling is an integral part of their culture, particularly for Yezidis because the religion is passed down orally. "If you talk and talk and talk you will normalize this [trauma] and you learn to control your feelings. . . . After the conflict has been dealt with in this way—and it's difficult, you have to do it over and over and over again—you can begin to think about the future, about going to school, having a business, et cetera."

On the eve of her journey, I asked Wadhah, the women whose parents fled from the Ottoman troops in what is now

Turkey, how she will be able to continue practicing the Yezidi religion as a refugee in America.

"We don't need a place to pray," she told me, as we sat together in her small home. "Just as long as you pray, then God hears you no matter where you are. We only pray quietly, even our family can't hear us praying, and when we pray we ask for the health and peace for seventy other religions, not just for the Yezidis.

"It's difficult to leave your land and the lands where you spent most of your time. If it wasn't for ISIS, I wouldn't want to leave, but after ISIS, I don't want to stay here." The Yezidi religion is closely linked to the land and the temples and shrines around Sinjar and Lallish. It's yet to be seen how the current migrations will influence the way Yezidism is practiced.

One of Wadhah's sons is already in America. When he left Iraq, he carried some small balls of sacred earth he had received at the temple in Lallish, and placed them in a purse that he took with him. This purse now hangs on the wall of his house in Texas and the family pray in front of it at sunrise and sunset.

--

After her return, Leila was accepted into her community straight-away. She and other survivors were taken to Lallish, where they were blessed in the spring and brought back into the religion. "It was very nice; we felt very comfortable there." As the trauma of what she had been through began to subside, she sank back into the rhythms of family life: playing with the children, doing housework, greeting guests, and speaking to her neighbors and friends. But months after her escape, she was still living in fear that ISIS would find her. Five months after Shakir's death, she left the camp and went to stay in a nearby town. "I was afraid I was in danger, that the people who were holding me would send someone to kidnap me," she said.

Now, she takes medicine so she can sleep at night and prefers to stay at home most of the time. She has lost a lot of weight. She says she would like to go to Germany. "It's no use staying here. No matter where we are, we think only about those of us who are still in captivity."

When she returned, her brother comforted her with words that offered immense relief. "Even though you were with ISIS, never think that you were married or were gone from us," he told her. "For us you are still the same girl as before."

Acknowledgments

This book was researched, written, and reported in 2015 and 2016, but builds on four years of independent, on the ground reporting in and around Iraqi Kurdistan. Any mistakes are my own. A huge thank you must go to Ibrahim and his kind (and growing) family who spent a lot of time explaining things to me, and showing me family photos and talking to me about life in Sinjar. A special thank you goes to the wonderful Layla (a different person from the "Leila" in the book) and Nawaf (Nawaf is a much better writer than I will ever be). Thanks to Alyas and his family, who put me up in their home, and Mahmood Zaki for all his help and research. Thanks to the staff at Yazda who let me wander in and out of their offices in Dohuk. Many of those who helped me with all stages cannot be named for security reasons. A debt of gratitude goes to Sherizaan Minwalla, Christine van den Toorn, Jan Kizilhan, and Allan Kaval for their important work on this topic, and deep thanks go to all the men and women who shared their stories with me, an experience that I hope didn't cause too much pain.

Isabel Coles and Patrick Osgood were extremely patient when it came to reading through drafts, giving advice, and talking through ideas. Sebastian Meyer is responsible for me being in Iraqi Kurdistan in the first place. Sofia Barbarani, Jodi Hilton, and Ali Arkady were excellent traveling companions who accompanied me on separate reporting trips to Sinjar and Dohuk, when some of the ideas for this book came about. Thank you to Patrick Cockburn for encouraging me to begin this project, to David Wastell for his help and advice as former foreign editor of *The Independent*, and to Colin Robinson of OR Books for his edits and suggestions.

Thanks to my brothers and to Alan Hill for putting up with me when I wasn't the best company, and also thanks to Adrian Otten, Roz Parr and Charlotte Abbott, Hanna, Jonas, and Kai Love Backman, Mark Russell and Oriole Parker-Rhodes, Maddii Lown and Owen Jones, Irene Dulz, Jared Levy, Georgia Horton, Debbie John, Matthew Boswell, Rawand Saeed, Hawre Khalid, Luke Coleman, Pishko Shamsi, Sareta Ashraph, Paulien Bakker, Jenna Krajeski, Sarah Baines, Noriko Hayashi, Daniele Raineri, Jessica S. Johnson, Brian Michael Lione, Katharyn Hanson,

Rawsht Twana, Barin and Pari Mohammed, JM Amberger, Jantine van Herwijnen, Ali Arafa, Melisande Genat, Arshed Baghdadi, and my Erbil housemates: Alice Martins, Cengiz Jar, Emily Kinskey, and Balint Szlanko.

Notes

1   The PKK and its sister groups, the YBS and YPG, have parallel female military structures that come under separate three letter acronyms. For the sake of clarity I'm just using the previous three to refer to both male and female units.

2   Author interview with Vian Dakhil, Yezidi KDP MP in the Iraqi Parliament. June 2016, Erbil, Iraqi Kurdistan.

3   V. Cetorelli, I. Sasson, N. Shabila, and G. Burnham, "Mortality and kidnapping estimates for the Yazidi population in the area of Mount Sinjar, Iraq, in August 2014: A retrospective household survey," *PLoS Med* 14, no.5 (2017): e1002297, doi.org/10.1371/journal.pmed.1002297.

4   Birgül Açikyildiz, *Yezidis: The History of a Community, Culture and Religion* (I.B Tauris), pp. 33–34.

5   Philip G. Kreyenbroek, *Yezidism – Its Background, Observances and Textual Tradition* (The Edwin Mellen Press, 1995), p. 45.

6   Ibid., p. 54. Quoting from Yezidi sacred texts that may be forgeries but appear to be based on oral accounts.

During author interviews with Yezidis, I heard different versions of this story; I also heard (in Kurdish) a telling of the story on a Yezidi TV show.

7   Author interview with Jan Kizilhan, a German-Yezidi professor of psychology and psychotherapy, who has treated many Yezidi women and helped to establish a program to bring them to Germany for treatment, Erbil, Iraqi Kurdistan, early 2016.

8   Kreyenbroek, p. 11.

9   John S. Guest, *Survival Among the Kurds: A History of the Yezidis* (Routledge, 1993), pp. 67, 136; Nelida Fuccaro, *The Other Kurds: Yazidis in Colonial Iraq* (I.B Tauris, 1999), p. 37.

10 Guest, p. 74; Fuccaro, p. 52.

11 Dr. Frederick Forbes, "A visit to the Sinjar hills in 1838, with some accounts of the sect of the Yezidis and of various places in the Mesopotamian desert, between the Tigris and Khabur," *The Journal of the Royal Geographical Society of London* 9 (1839): pp. 9–30.

12 Interviews with Melisande Genat, Stanford history PhD student and researcher, Erbil, Iraqi Kurdistan, December 2016, and Shamo Qassim, Yezidi historian, Dohuk, February 2017.

13 Genat interview.

14 Fuccaro, p. 151; Sara Pursley, "Lines Drawn on an Empty Map: Iraq's Borders and the Legend of the Artificial State," Jadaliyya, jadaliyya.com/pages/index/21780/lines-drawn-on-an-empty-map_iraq%E2%80%99s-borders-and-the.

15 Fuccaro, p. 49.

16 The district was home to 525 Jewish residents in late 1947. Genat interview; 1947 census.

17 "Manarat Madrasa Qutb al-Din Muhammad," https://archnet.org/sites/3839, and information from Dr. Katharyn Hanson, Smithsonian fellow and specialist in Mesopotamian archaeology.

18   Martin Smith, "The Rise of ISIS," *Frontline*, PBS, October 2014,
      pbs.org/wgbh/frontline/film/rise-of-ISIS/.

19   Human Rights Watch, "Genocide in Iraq: The Anfal Campaign
      against the Kurds," *Middle East Watch Report* (July 1993).

20   Fanar Haddad, *Sectarianism in Iraq: Antagonistic Visions of Unity*
      (Oxford University Press, 2011), p. 92.

21   Ibid., p. 93.

22   Ibid., p. 107. There has been debate over the impacts of Saddam's
      faith campaign;
      Rasha Al Aqeedi, "Hisba in Mosul: Systematic Oppression in the
      Name of Virtue," George Washington Program on Extremism
      (February 2016), p. 4.

23   United Nations High Commissioner for Refugees, "UNHCR's
      Eligibility Guidelines for Assessing the International Protection
      Needs of Iraqi Asylum-Seekers," Geneva (August 2007), p. 80.

24   Charles Tripp, *A History of Iraq* (Cambridge University Press,
      2010), p. 282.

25   Ibid.

26   Ibid., p. 287.

27   Ibid., p. 290.

28   Among Sinjari Yezidis, Yezidism has taken on an ethnic as well as
      religious definition in response to efforts to co-opt the Yezidis as
      Kurds or Arabs, and because they were persecuted as a religious group.
      Some Yezidis see themselves as Kurds, especially near Dohuk and in
      the Sheikhan area, while others do not. Yezidis from the Nineveh
      town of Bashiqa speak Arabic and not Kurdish. The attacks of 2014
      galvanized many Yezidis from Sinjar to move away from identifying
      as Kurdish because they were not protected by the KRG's security
      forces. Previously, KDP control of Sinjar was premised on providing
      the Yezidis with security, protection, education (in Kurdish), and

jobs in exchange for votes and an implicit agreement to identify as part of the larger Kurdish nationalist project. Kurdish politicians and officials vehemently reject the idea of a Yezidi (non-Kurdish) ethnic identity, partly because there are historical links and partly because the Yezidi rejection of Kurdish identity threatens the KRG's political hold on Sinjar, which is thought to sit on a huge and as yet untapped source of natural gas: in 2009, two international energy companies are believed to have conducted preliminary appraisal of the area, and at the time of writing, the entire Sinjar district is being actively marketed to oil companies for exploration by the KRG's Ministry of Natural Resources. The highly sensitive subject of ethnic identity cannot be discussed out of the context of the recent painful history, or out of the context of Iraq's disputed territory politics.

As Fanar Haddad states in his book Sectarianism in *Iraq: Antagonistic* Visions of Unity (although not writing about the Yezidis), "A group's sorrows are often key components of a group's identity markers or… its 'border guards.' They not only define who is a member and who is not, but they accentuate the divide between groups by presenting the other as an oppressor or an otherwise privileged group" (p. 176).

Most Yezidis accept some historical relation to Kurds, stating all Yezidis were Kurds or vice versa, wrote the authors of the PAX for Peace report, "Sinjar after ISIS: Returning to disputed territory." Yezidis affiliated both with Kurdish parties and with the pro-Baghdad Yezidi Movement for Reform and Progress gained representation on the Nineveh provincial council after 2013. But the pro-Baghdad party was challenged by "aggressive" KDP tactics such as "threats and arrests," according to the PAX report. "It should be noted that, under the KRG, Yezidis are considered as Kurds and therefore have no seat quota in Parliament in Erbil. This has weakened their ability to assert their identity within the framework of Kurdish politics." PAX for Peace, "Sinjar after ISIS: Returning to disputed territory," June 2016, p.11, paxforpeace.nl/stay-informed/press/press-release-sinjarafter-isis-returning-to-disputed-territory.

29   Author interview with anonymous UN political worker; Author interview with Christine van den Toorn, director of the Institute of Regional and International Studies at the American University of Iraq; Human Rights Watch, *On Vulnerable Ground: Violence Against Minority Communities in Nineveh Province's Disputed Territories,* November 10, 2009; Ann Scott Tyson, "Vying for a Voice, Tribe in North Iraq Feels Let Down," *Washington Post,* December 27, 2005.

30   UNAMI (United Nations Assistance Mission for Iraq), *Disputed Internal Boundaries: Sinjar district* 1 (2009): p. 7.

31   Author interview with anonymous UN political worker, January 2017.

32   Author interview with Michael Knights, August 2016, the Lafer Fellow at the Washington Institute for Near East Policy and a specialist in Iraq's military and security.

33   V. Cetorelli: "An estimated 3,100 . . . Yazidis were killed, with nearly half of them executed—either shot, beheaded, or burned alive—while the rest died on Mount Sinjar from starvation, dehydration, or injuries during the ISIS siege. The estimated number kidnapped is 6,800."

34   International Crisis Group, "Arming Iraq's Kurds: Fighting IS, Inviting Conflict," *Crisis Group Middle East Report* no. 158 (May 12, 2015): p. 11.

35   The White House, "Statement by NSC Spokesperson Ned Price on the Death of ISIL Deputy Leader Fadhil Ahmed al-Hayali," August 21, 2015, https://obamawhitehouse.archives.gov/the-press-office/2015/08/21/statement-nsc-spokesperson-ned-price-death-isil-deputy-leader-fadhil.

36   Arthur Quesnay, 'The Sunni Revolution and the Outburst of Community Divisions in Iraq," noria-research.com/wp-content/uploads/2015/07/ NORIA_IRAQ_SUNNI_REVOLUTION_QUESNAY_12_14-1.pdf, p. 6; Author interview with unnamed UN official (2017) expanded upon this theory, as did circumstantial evidence from an author interview with a prominent Anbari Sunni revolutionary (2014).

37   Ibid.

38   The date of the air strike is disputed but the broad details are the same in different testimonies.

39   Alissa J. Rubin, Tim Arango, and Helene Cooper, "US Jets and Drones Attack Militants in Iraq, Hoping to Stop Advance," *New York Times*, August 8, 2014, nytimes.com/2014/08/09/world/ middleeast/iraq.html?_r=0.

40   Aliza Marcus, *Blood and Belief: The PKK and the Kurdish fight for Independence* (New York University Press, 2011), p. 243.

41   Jenna Krajeski, "What the Kurds Want," *Virginia Quarterly Review* (Fall 2015).

42   Human Rights Watch, *Under Kurdish Rule: Abuses in PYD-run Enclaves of Syria*, June 19, 2014, https://www.hrw.org/report/2014/06/19/ under-kurdish-rule/abuses-pyd-run-enclaves-syria.

43   "Turks Claim PKK Front Offices Remain Open," *Public Library of US Diplomacy*, August 10, 2006, WikiLeaks, wikileaks.org/plusd/ cables/06ANKARA4608_a.html.

44   Author interview with General Aziz Waisi, Erbil, Iraqi Kurdistan, June 2016.

45   Human Rights Watch, *Iraq: Armed Groups Using Child Soldiers,* December 22, 2016, https://www.hrw.org/news/2016/12/22/ iraq-armed-groupsusing-child-soldiers-0.

46   Aaron Y. Zelin, "Al Qaeda in Iraq enters the Syrian conflict," *al-Wasat* (blog), https://thewasat.wordpress .com/?s=al+qaeda+in+iraq+enters+the+syrian+conflict.

47   Patrick Cockburn, "Al-Qa'ida opens a new front line," *The Independent*, May 1, 2012, independent.co.uk/news/world/middle-east/al-qaida-opens-a-new-front-line-7704341.html.

48   International Crisis Group, *Make or Break: Iraq's Sunnis and the State*, August 2013, p. 14.

49   Ibid., p. 15.

50   Iraq Body Count, "Iraqi Deaths From Violence 2003–2011," January 2, 2012, iraqbodycount.org/analysis/numbers/2011/; Norwegian Refugee Council, "Iraq: IDPS and their prospects for durable solutions," June 2011, internal-displacement.org/assets/library/Middle-East/Iraq/pdf/ Iraq-June2011-Brief.pdf.

51   International Crisis Group, *Make or Break*, p. 18.

52   Ibid., p. 8.

53   Ibid.

54   Michael Knights, *The ISIL's Stand in the Ramadi-Fallujah Corridor, Counter Terrorism Center at West Point*, May 2014.

55   Ibid.

56   Ibid. This report also includes an explanation on the relationship between ISIS and other rebels in Fallujah at the time.

57   Arthur Quesnay, *The Sunni Revolution and the Outburst of Community Divisions in Iraq*, http://www.noria-research.com/the-sunni-revolution-and-the-outburst-of-community-divisions-in-iraq/

58   International Crisis Group, *Fight or Flight: The Desperate Plight of Iraq's Generation 2000*, p. 14.

59   Irene Dulz, "The displacement of the Yezidis after the rise of ISIS in Northern Iraq," *Kurdish Studies* 4, no. 2: pp. 131–47.

60   Accounts of Yezidi interlocutors who passed through the corridor in August 2014 and the account of journalist Allan Kaval who was present.

61   "The Revival of Slavery Before the Hour," *Dabiq online ISIS magazine*, no. 4 (October 2014): https://clarionproject.org/docs/islamic-state-isis-magazine-Issue-4-the-failed-crusade.pdf.

62   Ibid.

63   Kecia Ali, *Sexual Ethics and Islam: Feminist Reflections on Qur'an, Hadith and Jurisprudence* (Oneworld Publications, 2016), p. 67.

64   Aymenn Jawad Al-Tamimi, *Unseen Islamic State Pamphlet on Slavery,* aymennjawad.org/2015/12/unseen-islamic-state-pamphlet-on-slavery.

65   Memri Islamic State, "(ISIS) Releases Pamphlet on Female Slaves," https://www.hrw.org/news/2015/09/05/slavery-isis-rules.

66   UN Commission for the Inquiry on the Syrian Arab Republic, *They Came to Destroy Us: ISIS Crimes against the Yezidis,* June 15, 2015, pp. 11–12.

67   "U.S. Military Conducts Airstrikes Near Sinjar, Irbil," defense .gov/News/Article/Article/603077.

68   Cathy Otten, "Letter from Sinjar: Convert or Die," *The American Scholar* (Spring 2016): theamericanscholar.org/convert-or-die/#. VUhVqJSiaJ.

69   Cathy Otten, "ISIL ex-prisoners: 'We were in a queue to be killed,'" Al Jazeera, November 30, 2015, aljazeera.com/news/2015/11/isil-prisoners-queue-killed-151129135126010.html.

70   U.S. Central Command, "Syrian Arab Coalition captured Da'esh headquarters," July 19, 2016, centcom.mil/MEDIA/PRESS-RELEASES/Press-Release-View/Article/925981/syrian-arab-coalition-captures-daesh-headquarters/.

71   UN Commission for the Inquiry on the Syrian Arab Republic, *They Came to Destroy Us,* p. 12.

72   Al-Tamimi, *Unseen Islamic State Pamphlet on Slavery.*

73   Ibid.

74   Ali, *Sexual Ethics,* p. 67.

75   Kecia Ali, "Redeeming Slavery: The 'Islamic State' and the Quest for Islamic Morality," mizanproject.org/journalpost/redeeming-slavery/:"If one accepts that IS' tactics are chosen in part for

the reaction they aim to provoke, media reaction to enslavement would seem to justify it."

76   Al-Tamimi, *Unseen Islamic State Pamphlet on Slavery.*

77   Ali, "Redeeming Slavery": "These documents disconcertingly juxtapose the stark and sometimes brutal claims of owners over slaves' bodies with pious concern for the enslaved people's human needs for food, clothing, and sex."

78   Aymenn Jawad Al-Tamimi, Archive of Islamic State Administrative Docs, "Notice on buying sex slaves, Homs province," http://www.aymennjawad.org/2016/01/archive-of-islamic-state-administrative-documents-1.

79   BBC World News, "Islamic State: Yazidi women tell of sex-slavery trauma," December 22, 2014, bbc.co.uk/news/world-middle-east-30573385.

80   "Zarqawi's pledge of allegiance to Al Qaeda," *Mu'asker al-Battar no. 21: scholarship.tricolib.brynmawr.edu/bitstream/handle/10066/4757/ZAR20041017P.pdf.*

81   "Islamic State in Iraq Execute Syrian Truck Drivers," liveleak .com/view?i=73e_1389191167&comments=1.

82   The story of Shakir's background and jihadi years comes from a variety of sources and their narratives have been cross-checked, but there are still points of confusion and debate surrounding his life and movements. This doesn't claim to be a definitive account. Leila's account of her enslavement and his injuries match the broad chronology outlined to me by other sources.

83   BBC World News, "Mount Sinjar: Islamic State siege broken, say Kurds," bbc.com/news/world-middle-east-30539170.

84   Stephen Kalin, "In Mosul Orphanage, Islamic State groomed child soldiers," Reuters, reuters.com/article/us-mideast-crisis-iraq-children-idUSKBN15W0OU.

85   Kreyenbroek, p. 111.

86   Patrick Cockburn, "The death sentence that drags Dua back into a bloody feud," independent.co.uk/news/world/middle-east/the-deathsentence-that-drags-dua-back-into-a-bloody-feud-1956187. html; author interviews.

87   Author interview, Ido's Babasheikh, Erbil, Iraqi Kurdistan, May 30, 2016.

88   Canada: Immigration and Refugee Board of Canada, *Iraq: Honour-based violence in the Kurdistan region; state protection and support services available to victims,* February 15, 2016, IRQ105424.E, refworld.org/docid/56d7f9974.html; author Interviews.

89   "Department of Defense Press Briefing by Pentagon Press Secretary Peter Cook in the Pentagon Briefing Room," May 9, 2016, defense.gov/News/Transcripts/Transcript-View/Article/755468/department-of-defense-press-briefing-by-pentagon-press-secretary-peter-cook-in.

90   Christine van den Toorn, Patrick Osgood, Rawaz Tahir, and staff of Iraq Oil Report, "Split over Sinjar Strategy leave town in IS control," November 8, 2015.

91   Dulz, Irene Dulz. "The displacement of the Yezidis after the rise of ISIS in Northern Iraq," Kurdish Studies, Volume 4, No. 2, pp. 131–147.Add quote from the report here in the endnotes: "An estimated 70–85% of the IDP population in Dohuk governorate (286,500 to 345,000) are Yezidis from Sinjar." p. 141

92   Ibid., p. 15.

93   Fehim Taştekin, "How Deep Is Turkey's Sinjar Entanglement?," al-monitor.com/pulse/originals/2017/03/turkey-iraqi-kurdistan-ankara-is-getting-entangled-sinjar.html.

94   United States Department of State, Bureau of Democracy, Human Rights, and Labor, Country Reports on Human Rights Practices for 2016, Iraq 2016 Human Rights Report, p. 26, https://www.state.gov/documents/organization/265710.pdf:

"KDP-run checkpoints—also restricted the transport of food, medicines and medical supplies, and other goods into Sinjar and Rabia Districts. NGO and diplomatic contacts stated the measures appeared to be aimed at limiting the influence of the PKK and their local affiliates, but they claimed unpredictability and the extent of the restrictions limited IDP returns to these areas."

95   Christine van den Toorn, "The Wars After the War for Sinjar: How Washington Can Avert a New Civil War," warontherocks. com/2016/06/the-wars-after-the-war-for-sinjar-how-washington-can-avert-a-new-civil-war/.

96   Isabel Coles, "Iraqi Yazidis take revenge as Islamic State atrocities unearthed," uk.reuters.com/article/us-mideast-crISIS-iraq-yazidis-idUSKBN0LE1YQ20150210.